Oct. 10-12
1997
1107
GRADE
"A"
Oct. 6-8
'95
DAYS
F DA!
Augustana College
Viking
Days
Oct.
10-12
1986
Viking
Days
Augustana College
Oct.
18-20
1985
Oct. 4 - 6
OCT.
12-15
19
67
Augustana
Viking Days '91
Oct. 11-13
I
Augie
SIOUX FALLS
SIOUX FALLS, S.D.
Augustana
KING DAYS
'04
AUGUSTANA
Viking
Days
1999
OCT. 1-3
2908
LEGE
G DAYS '02
Ultimate
It's a

Augustana at 150

Martin Luther once asked, "What do we older folks live for if not for the care of the young, to teach and train them?" The importance he placed on education has been a hallmark of the Lutheran Church for centuries, and has been – and continues to be – part of Augustana's calling as one of its 40 colleges and universities.

On Behalf of Augustana College

Editor and Project Director
Bob Preloger, Vice President for Marketing and Communications

Associate Editors
Kelly Sprecher, Director of Communications and Media Relations
Emily Drommerhausen '04, Director of College Events

Contributors
Dr. Lynwood Oyos, professor emeritus of history; Dr. Joyce Nelson, professor emeritus of nursing; Dr. Harold "Doc" Krueger, professor emeritus of music; Dr. Ken Kessinger '49, professor emeritus of HPER and coach; Dr. Sandra Looney '62, professor of English; Dr. Arlen Viste, professor emeritus of chemistry; Dr. Gary Olson, professor emeritus of history; Dr. Roy Kintner, professor emeritus of chemistry; Mel Klein, retired, men's basketball coach and director of development; Bruce Conley, retired, director of news information; Amanda Jensen '09, archives collection, Center for Western Studies; The Rev. Dave Johnson '56; President Ralph Wagoner; President Bruce Halverson '66; President Rob Oliver

Additional Sources
Through Trials and Triumphs. A History of Augustana College by Dr. Donald Sneen, 1985; *A History of Augustana College* by Dr. Emil Erpestad, 1955; *From the Archives, Volume I* by Dr. Helmer M. "Pat" Blegen, ca. 1970; *Augustana Today; Edda; The Mirror*

Photo Credits
Johnny Sundby '90; T. J. Nelson '05; Duane Waack; Steve Woit; archives collection, Center for Western Studies; Dave Tunge, Dakota Aerials

On Behalf of Lifetouch Inc.

Executive Publisher
Paul Harmel '72, Chairman and CEO

Publisher
Lifetouch Inc.
Office of Communications
11000 Viking Drive
Eden Prairie, Minnesota 55344
952.826.4000
lifetouch.com

Executive Director
Kelvin W. Miller

Project Director
Michael Faust

Writer and Editor
Elizabeth Sietsema

Design and Art Direction
Jacob Murphy

Printing
Lifetouch Services, Loves Park, Illinois

Augustana College
2001 South Summit Avenue
Sioux Falls, South Dakota 57197
605.274.0770
augie.edu

ISBN 978-0-931170-11-9
Printed in the United States

Contents

Augustana at 150! Throughout the pages of this book, we have attempted to tell the story of our College, to chronicle the very heart and soul of its history. Each time we delve into the backstory of Augustana, we are reminded of the fortitude of our Norwegian founders—their vision, their courage and strength, their sheer determination, and the *faith* that moved them forward despite innumerable challenges. A mission statement then could have read much as ours does today:

Inspired by Lutheran scholarly tradition and the liberal arts, Augustana provides an education of enduring worth that challenges the intellect, fosters integrity and integrates faith with learning and service in a diverse world.

Before settling in Sioux Falls, the College moved five times. As the pioneers moved westward, so did the institution—its mission as a college of the Church always at the forefront. Think of it . . . think of the determination and effort it took to pack up and move a school as people in the fledgling Midwest were struggling to settle and adapt. Despite the difficulties, and the turmoil that often accompanied them, Augustana persevered and, today, it is one of the premier church-related colleges in the United States. Augustana has survived because of the indomitable spirit of its people who believed it was possible—the courageous souls who championed its mission and the countless loyal and dedicated students and families, faculty and staff, and alumni and friends who have held Augustana close in their hearts . . . and continue to do so.

I share these words from the 2010 Sesquicentennial Convocation: "We celebrate and honor our past, the legacy of those who have gone before us to create the *Augustana Like Always* that we have come to love. As we embark on our next 150 years, we boldly set out together each day, creating the *Augustana Like Never Before* to send forth men and women equipped with minds and hearts to change the world." Thanks be to God.

Yours, for Augustana,

Robert C. Oliver
President of the College

Setting Roots in America

America first loomed on the horizon for Scandinavians in the early 1800s. Talk trickled their way, telling of broader religious tolerance and the possibilities of land ownership in this faraway place. That appealed to adventurous malcontents and religious dissidents who were seeking freedom from the constraints of the Norwegian state church, escape from poor economic conditions, and who were eager to become their own landlords.

At the urging of Norwegian Quakers, a man named Cleng Peerson came to America in the early 1820s to seek prospects for settlement. Upon his return to Norway, armed with a positive report of his visit, it was decided that Peerson should make the necessary arrangements for settling the emigrants. He chose a location in New York that he thought would be ideal. However, the countryside and economics of the area proved difficult for the new settlers; thus, their discord made life difficult for Peerson.

So, in 1833, determined to find a better home for his fellow Norwegians, his travels eventually took him to Illinois, a region of rich soil and equitable land prices. Finding this prairie place near Chicago, Peerson returned to New York with rave reviews and sound reasons for families to venture forth and resettle there. The word went out about the openness and promise of prairie life. Resident numbers soon were increasing, eventually branching into neighboring parts, including what is now Wisconsin. The area became an entry hub for an influx of Norwegians when messages of the good life reached Norway telling of great freedom and opportunity, often backed up with enclosed sums of money.

In the 1830s and the 1840s, not only were the Scandinavians putting down roots in the Midwest, but there was also a shift taking place in America. People were moving in from other parts of the country and settling down, building churches, and bringing in members. Religion was very important in the lives of the immigrants, many of whom, of course, had left their homeland for freedom from a "high and mighty" state church. If they were not provided for, it was feared they would be lost to Lutheranism. Organizing the frontier church was not without difficulty. Communication and travel were problematic. "Synods" were organized by pastors and congregations for convenience. There was divisiveness as to orthodox, liberal, or middle of the road, and adherence to the Lutheran confessions.

There were concerns relative to education as well. The Scandinavian immigrant families brought many children with them. Schooling in America was believed to be not suitable for Scandinavian children. Institutions of learning began to appear, their success often beset by financial problems, leadership tensions, influence for Scandinavian language and literature, and adherence to the Word and the Augsburg Confession, the succinct doctrinal message of Lutheranism.

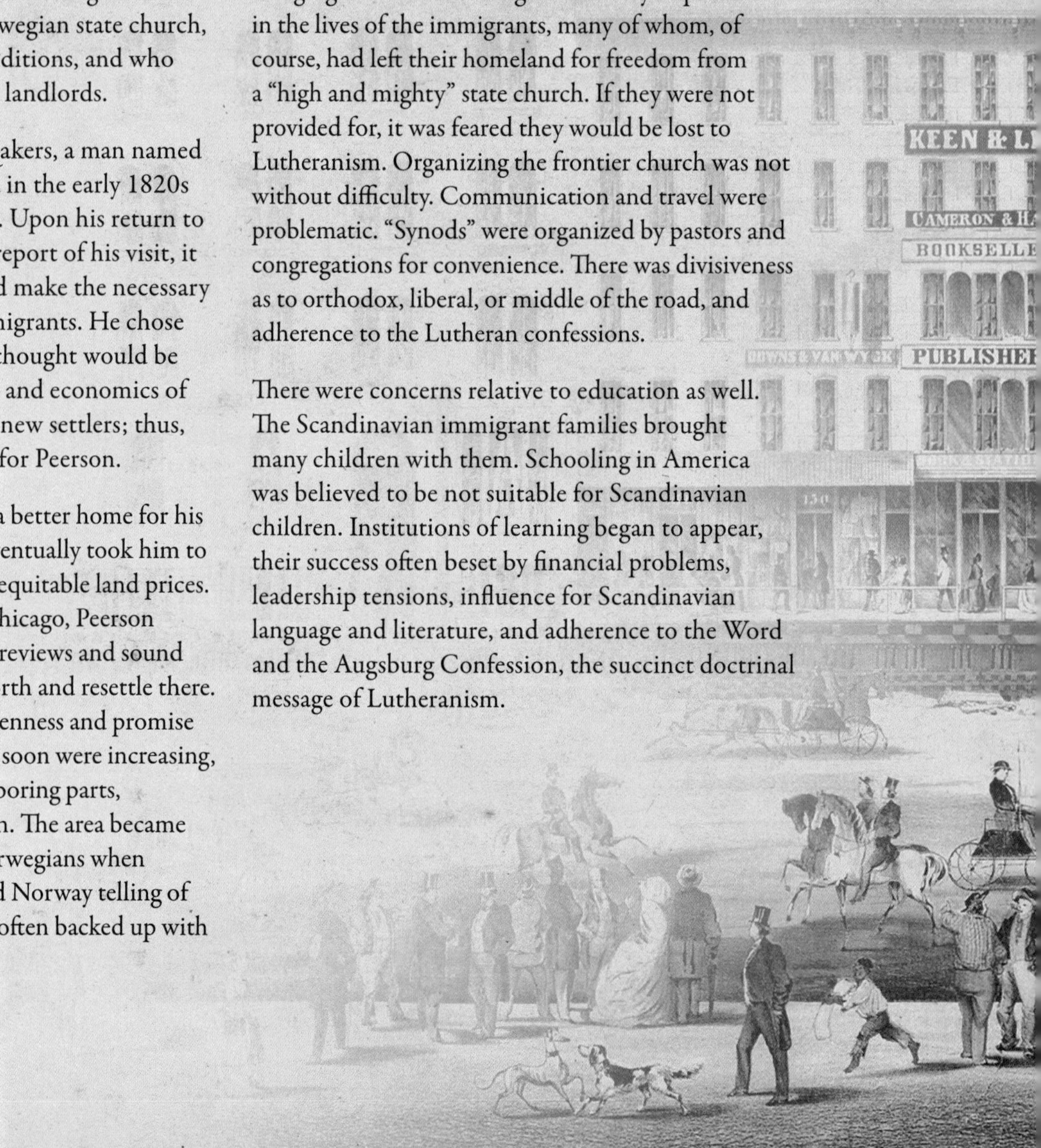

1860, Raising a block of brick buildings on Lake Street, Chicago

1863-1869 The Rev. Tuve N. Hasselquist, the second president, convinces the Church that the seminary should move to Paxton.

1860-1863 The Rev. Lars P. Esbjorn is the first president of Augustana Seminary.

The Norwegian Augustana moves to Marshall, Wisconsin, and is named Augsburg Seminary and Marshall Academy.

1869

A COLLEGE MOVES WEST 1860-1890

1860

The Scandinavians open Augustana Seminary in Chicago on September 1, based on the Augsburg Confession—*Confessio Augustana*—Augustana, the Latin for Augsburg.

1865

The seminary receives its official charter as Augustana College and Theological Seminary.

1863

Augustana Seminary moves to Paxton, Illinois, when a

1869-1870 The Rev. August Weenaas serves only one year as the school's third president in Marshall. He eventually becomes the first president of Augsburg College, Minneapolis.

1870-1876 John J. Anderson, principal of Marshall Academy, is historically considered the fourth president.

1889-1890 The Rev. Christian S. Salvesen serves as the seventh president of Augustana College.

1875

The Swedish Augustana relocates from Paxton to its present-day location in Rock Island, Illinois.

1888

Henry M. Solem is awarded the first bachelor of arts degree.

1890 STUDENT ENROLLMENT - 116

1881

Augustana Seminary and Academy opens in Beloit, Iowa.

1884

The academy moves to Canton, Dakota Territory, and is named Augustana College.

1889

Lutheran Normal School is built in Sioux Falls.

South Dakota becomes a state on November 2.

1876-1884 The Rev. David Lysnes, the fifth president, serves in Marshall, Wisconsin, and then in Beloit, Iowa.

1884-1889 Professor Matthew D. Miller is the sixth president of the school in Canton.

1860-1890

A College Moves West

On September 1, 1860, Augustana Seminary opened in the Norwegian Lutheran Church on Franklin Street in Chicago, offering courses in theology and preparatory academy curriculum. It was a joint venture of Swedes and Norwegians in the area that followed the founding of the Augustana Synod [Scandinavian Evangelical Lutheran Augustana Synod in North America] in June of 1860. The Rev. Lars Esbjorn, formerly the Scandinavian professor at Illinois State University, was the designated theological professor and also served as president. His tenure was burdensome. There was a lack of qualified faculty, recruitment of students was difficult due to the Civil War and opposing views on slavery, and fiscal matters were tenuous at best. Most difficult for him was when the synod announced that it had made a decision to move Augustana Seminary to Paxton, Illinois.

Having devoted himself to this struggling ministry, and with an increasing desire to return to Sweden following numerous family tragedies, Esbjorn resigned in 1863 to take a parish in Sweden.

The seminary's move to Paxton in 1863 was precipitated by offers of land from a railroad that was eager to attract settlers, so eager in fact that the synod was offered a premium for land sold. At that time, the Swedes dominated the seminary. The Rev. August Weenaas, one of the Norwegian professors, was straightforward in his opinion that the Norwegians should separate from the Swedes and, as a result, he made every effort to relocate the Norwegians to another place. In 1869, an amicable agreement was reached and Weenaas moved the Norwegian segment to Marshall, Wisconsin, a few miles northeast of Madison.

To distinguish itself from the Swedish Augustana Seminary, and after an existing academy was absorbed as part of the relocation transaction, the Norwegian contingent was now officially Augsburg Seminary and Marshall Academy. Not unlike any other emerging institution, it had its share of problems. Financial support was inadequate and Weenaas did not favor the academy's association with the seminary. He was a theologian and not much interested in the academy's educational mission. Differences eventually led Weenaas and the seminary students to move from the campus. In 1872, the theological seminary moved to Minneapolis, while the academy remained in Marshall. With the academy facing heavy financial burdens, the Norwegian Augustana Synod, at a board of trustees meeting in Milwaukee in 1880, had to make a decision—what to do with the academy.

As chance would have it, an extraordinary gentleman, who had migrated from Norway, appeared on the scene. His name was James Wahl, a commissioner of immigration for Dakota Territory. Upon arriving in the United States, he had enrolled in school in La Crosse, Wisconsin, to learn the English language. Having command of English proved very advantageous for Wahl as he traveled about the Midwest, greeting Norwegians as they arrived via the railroads. He served as a translator, and, thus, he gave the appearance of a representative of the government and the railroads.

Wahl happened to be in Milwaukee when the Norwegian Augustana Synod Board of Trustees was meeting to discuss the future of the school. He went to the meeting and convinced the synod to move the academy to the Big Sioux River Valley in Dakota Territory. He argued that Norwegian settlers were migrating to the burgeoning western frontier. As a result of his persuasive oratory, the synod approved a move "to a suitable place in the West."

Augustana Seminary, Paxton, Illinois

Norwegian Lutheran Church, Chicago, Illinois

Augsburg Seminary and Marshall Academy, Marshall, Wisconsin

Augustana Seminary and Academy, Beloit, Iowa

James Wahl

Settling on a site was cause for debate, but it was finally decided that the school would locate in Beloit, Iowa, and open for spring term 1881. Moving the academy from Marshall proved challenging. Not only was the school property to be moved, but there was the matter of the school's very large bell, which had been donated by a Norwegian immigrant farmer, Endre Endresen Eidsvaag, during the academy's first year in Marshall. To further complicate matters, there were months of crippling prairie snowstorms. In order to meet the opening deadline, Wahl approached Milwaukee Road [railroad] officials and asked for help with the move.

The stay in Beloit was short-lived. With student enrollment increasing, it became apparent that there was a need for expanded facilities. A group of Dakota Territory citizens in Canton pooled their resources and acquired the newly constructed Naylor House Hotel. The building was offered to the Norwegian Augustana Synod with the conditions that the school move from Beloit to Canton, and that a college be established.

While in Beloit, the former Marshall school reclaimed the name, Augustana Seminary and Academy. Not until 1884 was the academy's move to Canton completed, where it became Augustana College. The seminary remained in Beloit until it moved to Augsburg Seminary, Minneapolis, in 1890.

ca. 1905, Augustana College, Canton

VISIONARY LEADERSHIP 1890-1920

1890-1916 The Rev. Anthony G. Tuve becomes the eighth president of Augustana College at age 26. He serves for 26 years, the longest of any president.

1894

1895

The Augustana College Association assumes maintenance, operations, and finances of the school, beneficial because it is top-of-mind for members of the association, mostly local and loyal supporters.

1901

Ole Rolvaag, author of *Giants in the Earth*, graduates from the academy.

1903

First permanent building is added to the Canton campus.

President Anthony Tuve resigns.

1915

1918-1920 **Professor Hans S. Hilleboe**, president of Lutheran Normal School prior to the merger, is the tenth president of Augustana College.

The first college paper, *The Augustana*, is published.

1908

1920 STUDENT ENROLLMENT - 242

1905

Ladies Hall (women's residence) is built at Lutheran Normal School.

1918

Augustana College, Canton, moves to Sioux Falls following its merger with Lutheran Normal School. On August 14, its official name becomes Augustana College and Normal School.

1916

1916-1918 **Dr. Paul M. Glasoe** is the College's ninth president, serving the last two years the College is in Canton.

Class of 1904 in Canton

1890–1920

Visionary Leadership

Moving Augustana westward toward an increasing Norwegian population in the Midwest was not yet living up to the rosy picture painted by James Wahl. Life in middle America, where a great segment of the people had settled and become farmers, was a challenge for a number of reasons. In the late 1890s and early in the new century, poor weather conditions prevailed over long periods, the economy vacillated, the railroads that had played a large role in settling the region were now looking out for themselves—and the immigrant generation of Norwegians began trailing off in separate directions. Though most were suffering many of the same ups and downs, there were those who also had a deep-rooted interest in retaining the old traditions, while others were struggling to adapt to their new homeland and manage everyday life.

Ethnic groups sprang up, hoping to shore up the Norwegian heritage. However, the advent of World War I in 1914 greatly diminished foreign ethnicity when a law was passed that required patriotism be taught and prohibited foreign language instruction. And, a new generation of young people was emerging, children of immigrants who wanted to be Americans—to speak in English, not in the language of the old country. Norwegian culture, language, and literature began to take a back seat as the Church recognized that it and its educational institutions must adapt to worship and instruction in English.

The College was not immune to the effects of all of this. However, it had the good fortune to have Anthony G. Tuve as its leader, a capable and dedicated man who came on board as president in 1890. Tuve adeptly guided the College through the economic and cultural stresses of the 1890s. There was a depression. There was a drought and a grasshopper plague, but his largest crisis came in 1894. The United Church, of which Augustana was part, was having its own problems, bickering over property of its educational institutions. The church wanted Augustana closed; there would be no further financial support. If Tuve wanted to continue to operate, he would have to be responsible. And operate he did. His vision and multiple talents carried Augustana through the financial "brink." Rather than let the College fail, he rallied loyal friends and he, himself, gave of his own funds.

Concern about the school led to the formation of the Augustana College Association in February 1895 by pastors and congregational representatives in the Canton area. The association assumed maintenance, operations, and finances of the school. The management, which continued as long as Augustana remained in Canton, was beneficial because it was top-of-mind for members of the association, mostly local and loyal supporters.

Lutheran Normal School, Sioux Falls

AUGUSTANA

Women's Residence, Canton

In response to area interests and with a desire to grow enrollment, in the early 1900s Augustana, originally established to train men for the ministry, undertook an effort to broaden the curriculum. Extracurricular activities emerged along with additional academic disciplines. Student numbers increased. This necessitated additional faculty and created need for more facilities for a college that was basically operating out of one building—the Naylor House Hotel in downtown Canton. In 1902, the Naylor House was moved to an east-side location in Canton and Augustana's first permanent structure was built there the following year.

Anthony Tuve submitted his resignation as president of Augustana in 1915. He consented to an additional year as president while a search was conducted for his successor. In 1916, having competently guided the College through 26 up-and-down years at great personal sacrifice, he returned to classroom teaching.

The Norwegian Lutheran Church of America merger in 1917 brought Augustana College at Canton and Lutheran Normal School at Sioux Falls into the same synod. The Lutheran Normal School had been established in 1889 to train teachers. To more effectively fulfill and strengthen the educational mission of the Norwegian Lutheran Church, it was decided by church leaders that Augustana College in Canton and the Lutheran Normal School in Sioux Falls should become one. There was debate as to the site for the merged campus. Sioux Falls city and business leaders lobbied hard for the College to be located there. The choice rested with the Church. Ultimately, its adopting resolutions designated Sioux Falls; on August 14, 1918, the school's official name became Augustana College and Normal School. The consolidation led the way for Augustana to become a fully accredited senior college.

Professor Hans S. Hilleboe, president of Lutheran Normal School prior to the merger, was named acting president. He was very adept at communicating the new school's mission and needs. Faculty and students from the College and the Normal School fell in line and supported efforts toward beginning to build a strong educational institution. Despite opposing views on the merging of Augustana College and Lutheran Normal School, the strengths each institution brought to the table were indisputable. United, the two could be stronger than one, with greater opportunity for growth and development.

1908, The first Augustana College band

1909, An early choir of faculty and students

CHAPEL
AUGUSTANA COLLEGE
CANTON, S.D.

SUMMIT
AUGUSTANA

1915, Baseball team, Augustana College, Canton

ca. 1910, Summit Avenue trolley by Lutheran Normal School, Sioux Falls

1915, Postcard depicting Ladies Hall and Old Main

Men's Residence, Canton

1920-1928 The Rev. Dr. Charles Orin Solberg is the eleventh president. Before coming to Augustana, Dr. Solberg was president of the English Association of the Norwegian Lutheran Church of America.

BUILDING A CAMPUS 1920-1940

1921

The Augustana Concert Choir is organized by Dr. Carl Youngdahl, who serves as its director until 1953.

1922

Augustana is instrumental in starting the South Dakota Symphony Orchestra.

The Augustana Student Association is organized and is responsible for overseeing student activities.

The College joins the South Dakota Intercollegiate Conference. The name, Vikings, is adopted and the colors blue and gold are chosen.

1923

Julia Mary Tisthammer receives the first bachelor of arts degree from the combined Augustana College and Normal School.

An orchestra is organized in the fall by Marie Toohey and makes its debut March 31, 1924.

1924

Augustana receives its charter as the 100th member of Pi Kappa Delta, national forensic honor society.

First college homecoming. Louise Solberg is queen.

1929-1932 The Rev. Dr. Ove J. H. Preus is installed as the thirteenth president on October 25, 1929; the stock market collapses on October 29. Prior to Augustana, Dr. Preus served as president of the Eastern District of the Norwegian Lutheran Church.

Homecoming is now recognized as Viking Days.

1929

1932-1943 The Rev. Dr. Clemens Granskou is Augustana's fourteenth president, having previously served in the same capacity at Waldorf College, Forest City, Iowa.

BUILDING A CAMPUS 1920-1940

1928

The *Edda* yearbook is first published.

College broadcasts begin from radio station KSOO.

1931

Augustana receives North Central accreditation.

Arthur Larson is named the first Rhodes Scholar.

Coach Leonard "Lefty" Olson arrives to lead the athletic program.

1928-1929 The Rev. Dr. H. J. Glenn, member of the College's board of directors, agrees to serve as the twelfth president for one year and then returns to his previous position as pastor of First Lutheran Church, Sioux Falls.

1932

Augustana is almost closed by the Church's board of education due to lack of funds.

1934

Joe Foss, eventual WWII flying ace, governor of South Dakota, and first commissioner of the American Football League, enrolls as a freshman.

Augustana and other denominational colleges in South Dakota receive financial assistance from Homestake Mining Company of Lead.

1937

Dedication of the long-awaited gymnasium-chapel-auditorium is June 8.

1938

Dr. Albert Hoyem establishes an aviation program.

1938 STUDENT ENROLLMENT - 429

1939

Crown Prince Olav and Crown Princess Martha of Norway visit the Augustana campus in June.

Ole the Viking makes first appearance as the official College mascot; the initial design is submitted by Austin Kilian '42.

1940

All men of military age are required to register for the draft. Students sign pledge refusing to participate in armed conflict outside U.S. boundaries. With the bombing of Pearl Harbor in 1941, the pledge is no longer realistic.

1920, Construction of the Administration building

1920-1940

Building A Campus

Augustana began to experience winds of change when Charles Orin Solberg assumed the presidency in 1920. Solberg was probably the most influential in changing the direction of the College. He came armed with extensive experience in parish ministry, college teaching, and church administration. His education was non-Scandinavian and his views Americanized. While President Tuve had supported vocational courses, President Solberg advocated more liberal arts curricula. Under his tutelage, the school's transformation to a credible American Lutheran four-year liberal arts college began. English was established as the language for learning and priorities were initiated for moving the school forward. Added impetus was completion in 1920 of the first new structure on the Sioux Falls campus, the Administration building.

President Solberg's leadership was not without challenges, however. He came on board when the advent of such things as radio, movies, automobiles, mail-order catalogs, and installment purchasing were changing the lives of people on the Plains. Industry was flourishing while agriculture and area farmers were struggling to recover from faltering economic optimism in grain markets in 1920. Student enrollment suffered. Money was hard to come by, funds for public education were reduced, and Norwegian ethnicity was transitioning to Americanization, all of which impacted the College.

Administration

Top priority for Dr. Solberg was to make Augustana College and Normal School academically strong. He created departments, many in the humanities and sciences. In the early 1920s, the academy's campus at Canton remained active, the result of which created a great deal of competition between the two institutions. Through masterful guidance, Solberg appeased those on both campuses. Despite shaky money matters, he began to develop a well-educated faculty. Enrollment increased by nearly three times and student activities and organizations sprang up. In 1926, solid endowment fund-raising moved the College closer toward President Solberg's goal of obtaining accreditation by the North Central Association of Colleges and Secondary Schools. He was laying the groundwork for Augustana to become a strong liberal arts Lutheran college in America.

In 1928, Dr. Solberg was offered a position at Chicago Lutheran School and took leave of Augustana. An immediate search for a new leader was not fruitful, so it was decided to call Dr. H. J. Glenn, pastor at First Lutheran Church in Sioux Falls, as interim president. He had been closely associated with the College as a member of its board of directors and was of the same mind as Dr. Solberg. Glenn's attitude seemed to be that he was going to take advantage of his interim status and make his mark before returning to his pastorate at First Lutheran Church. He dismissed a number of old-line staff members and hired faculty with Ph.D.s—including Ingvald Hauge, John Froemke, and Albert Hoyem who joined the intellectual Helmer "Pat" Blegen, the standard-bearer of excellence who had arrived at Augustana in 1927.

The experienced churchman, Dr. Ove J. H. Preus, who earlier had declined a call to Augustana College, reconsidered and was installed on October 25, 1929, just days before "Black Tuesday," the day the stock market collapsed marking the beginning of the Great Depression. He came from a long line of clergymen and was well educated, being both pastor and trained lawyer. He was also patient and dedicated, which served him and Augustana well while the College grappled with the impact of the nation's catastrophic depression, droughts, and insect infestations, all of which were front and center for people of the Plains. Though student numbers remained fairly steady, the Preus era struggled with continuous financial concerns. Faculty went without pay and building plans were put on hold. Notwithstanding, in 1931, citing progress in developing a stronger faculty, the quality of Augustana graduates, the excellent leadership of President Preus, and the stability of income provided by the Church, the North Central Association of Colleges and Secondary Schools recommended Augustana for accreditation.

A variety of activities and organizations emerged in the late '20s and early '30s. Publications such as the *Edda* yearbook began to appear, the debate team was outstanding, and science, music, and theatre groups were gaining recognition. Religious activities were prominent. Graduate Arthur Larson received the prestigious Rhodes Scholarship. And when Leonard "Lefty" Olson came to Augustana in 1931 as director of athletics and head coach, it was a new day for Viking athletics.

A decision in 1925 had placed joint operation of Augustana Academy, and its two-year normal training program in Canton, and Augustana College, Sioux Falls, under the watchful eye of the Augustana College Association. In the spring of 1932, Dr. Preus received a call to become president of Luther College. Prior to his departure from Augustana, however, he had determined that it was no longer fiscally responsible for the College and Augustana Academy to operate under a sole administration, feeling there was a very real possibility both schools might fail. The Norwegian Lutheran Church of America dictated that an Academy Association be formed. President Preus skillfully waded through debates with both institutions relative to property ownership, assets, and liabilities with a compromise ultimately reached. Augustana Academy, now separated from Augustana College, continued to operate successfully as a church-related academy in Canton until it closed in 1971.

Successor to Preus, Clemens Granskou was well qualified when he moved into the president's office in 1932. His military background and his missionary, educational, and administrative experiences made him well suited for his role in leading the College. With the ongoing depression and severe Great Plains drought, economic times were grim, all of which affected the mostly rural membership of the Norwegian Lutheran Church of America and its educational institutions. Despite frugality, survival of the Church's senior colleges was in doubt, Augustana

among them. In 1934, an appeal to Homestake Mining Company of Lead, South Dakota, for financial assistance resulted in a generous donation. Over the next four years, Augustana continued to receive annual grants from the company that eventually would help put the College on a more sound financial footing.

Though times were difficult, enrollment was increasing which, in turn, required additions to the faculty. To economize and meet that need, curriculum changes were kept to a minimum, courses were dropped or study requirements reduced. Some members of the faculty arranged loans from personal insurance policies to contribute financially toward support of the College. President Granskou did his part by teaching religion, in addition to his administrative duties.

Staff and students shared a common loyalty to Granskou and his leadership skills. He had great rapport with students, most of whom viewed their education as a privilege. They came from families who had not been able to attend college. They were conservative and traditional—and his counsel, wisdom, and accessibility were qualities to appreciate. A quote from the 1941 *Edda* reads, "Augustana is a growing institution and as such requires a president who takes the college's growing pains in stride, gives direction to its growth, and promotes the welfare of students and faculty alike. The college presidency calls for a man who can satisfy the constituency, keep the students well in hand, and regulate the delicate constitutions of faculty members—all while keeping within the budget. Augustana has just such a versatile diplomat in its virile, stocky president, C. M. Granskou."

Granskou also felt that relationships between the College and the wider community were beneficial. He was very good at developing and fostering local ties as well as strengthening those within the church constituency. He said, "The Church must enter positively into the fields of higher education . . . Religion and education are the two greatest forces in human life. The two belong together."

1925, Women's Basketball

1920, First football team

1924, Augustana Choir, directed by Dr. Carl Youngdahl from 1921 to 1953

GROUND FLOOR
SIOUX FALLS

1925, Homecoming

Augustana
Home Coming
VIKINGS vs HURON
October 17, 1925
SENIOR
SIOUX FALLS

1926, All-school photograph

1923, Spring tour includes 12 stops across Iowa, Minnesota, Nebraska, and South Dakota

1927, CHOIR TOUR IN WESTERN SOUTH DAKOTA

Vol. XII

GREATEST NUMBER IN HIS…

Granskou Assumes Duties a…

TO BE INSTALLED OCTOBER…

Fills Position Left Vacant by Preus; Is Highly Qualified

Experience in Aviation, Missions Add Color to His Career

Students of the college were greeted by a new face in the president's office when they returned this fall. This is the face of Pres. C. M. Granskou, formerly president of Waldorf college, Forest City, Iowa. Pres. Granskou was elected to this position at a meeting of the Augustana college association held in Minneapolis, June 6. He succeeds Dr. O. J. H. Preus, who came to Augustana in 1929 and who has been called to fill a similar position at Luther college, Decorah, Iowa.

The new president has had many and varied experiences, which include military patrol service with the U. S. naval aviation corps, service as a U. S. air mail pilot, missionary experiences in the heart of China, educational activity at home and abroad, and service as a college professor and executive.

Well Qualified

Pres. Granskou comes to Augustana highly recommended as a college administrator and as a sympathetic student of college problems. Since 1929 he has been president of Waldorf college where he has succeeded in raising a large endowment fund under the most trying conditions. In his work at this Iowa institution, he has succeeded in building a large student body and an excellently qualified faculty. The student enrollment there last year was the largest in history. Additional accreditation with the North Central Association of colleges and secondary schools was another of the splendid achievements which Pres. G…

CLEMENS M. GRANSKOU

Two Mus…

gustana Mirror

AN ALL-AMERICAN PAPER, 1932

College, Sioux Falls, S. D., Thursday, September 15, 1932

No. 9

Y OF SCHOOL ENROLL FOR COLLEGE COURSES

ew Augustana President

Domsitz to Arrange Viking Day Events; Committees Chosen

Mickelson, Benard to Aid In Planning Many New Features

At the first meeting of the student association held during the chapel period Friday morning, September 9, Myron Domsitz was elected general chairman of the Viking Day festivities to be held October 15. As such, he will arrange for the scheduling of activities and organizing committees for the annual Augustana homecoming.

Especially significent in this year's program will be the installation services of Rev. C. M. Granskou to the presidency of Augustana college. A formal installation service is being planned by the committee appointed by Mr. Domtz.

Chief among those chosen to fill sponsible positions are Roger Berd, parade chairman, and Sigfried ickelson, director of publicity.

A departure from former Viking y programs will be the final initin meeting held for the freshmen ween the halves of the evening foot- game. The Vikings are scheduled meet the Yankton college Greyds in the traditional homecoming ball game. Further plans will be unced in the next issue of the or.

Holds High Position

MARTIN L. COLE

Prof. Cole Named New College Dean

Prof. Martin L. Cole of the history department will fill the new position of Dean of Augustana college. As such he will be responsible for the administration of the program of instructional work. It will be his duty to study the curriculum and recommend major changes for the coordination of the work of the college departments.

In addition Prof. Cole will be responsible for making a systematic study of the personal problems of student life, taking into ...

Record Number of Freshmen Brings 27 Per Cent Increase, Accreditation Attracts Many

Extension Clases Will Be Organized On Enlarged Scale

Highly Qualified Staff to Instruct—Wlil Organize Soon

In response to numerous requests from people who find it impossible to attend the regular college classes, Augustana will offer extension work this year on a wider scale than ever before. This plan places the facilities of the entire institution at the disposal of all those who enroll for this work. According to Prof. W. P. Hieronymus, director, the regular classes will meet in the parlors of the First Lutheran church, beginning some time late in September.

Offer Varied Program

The purpose of the extension department is to accommodate teachers who wish to work for the renewal of a certificate or for a higher one while still continuing teaching, for persons who wish to secure credit toward a bachelor's degree, or for anyone interested in broadening his cultural outlook.

Classes will be given in sociology, economics, psychology, foreign languages, English, history, art, education, public speech, and music. In general, one semester hour of credit will be given for any course pursued for seven weeks, meeting one evening a week.

Instructors Highly Qualified

Large Group From City

Upperclassmen Transfer from Twelve Colleges and Normals

The greatest number of students in the history of Augustana college registered this fall, according to Prof. John G. Berdahl, registrar.

The phenomenal increase in the number of students has taken place primarily in the freshman class where the percentage has been steadily mounting until there are approximately 27 per cent more freshmen than last year. The new student total approaches this mark due to an influx of students from Waldorf and other colleges.

Many Upper Classmen Back

Figures are not yet complete on enrollment for the entire college but as the Mirror goes to press, the mark was far above last year's and will undoubtedly set a new all time record. Junior and senior students have come back in far greater numbers than were expected.

Especially encouraging in the growth this year is the great number of Sioux Falls high school graduates in the freshman class. Nearly three times as many as in any previous year have registered. Also noteworthy is the number of junior colleges, normal schools, and senior colleges represented in the registration. Waldorf college heads the list, with the four South Dakota normal schools and Augustana academy following closely. Also represented are St. Olaf, Sioux Falls, Wayne Normal, Concordia, University of South Dakota, University of Iowa, Minot State Teacher's, Steven's college for women, St. Thomas, and St. Paul Luther college.

1933, Orchestra, directed by Dr. Richard Guderyahn from 1927 to 1959

1935, Coach Lefty's "Leftymen" take the field

1938, Augustana College

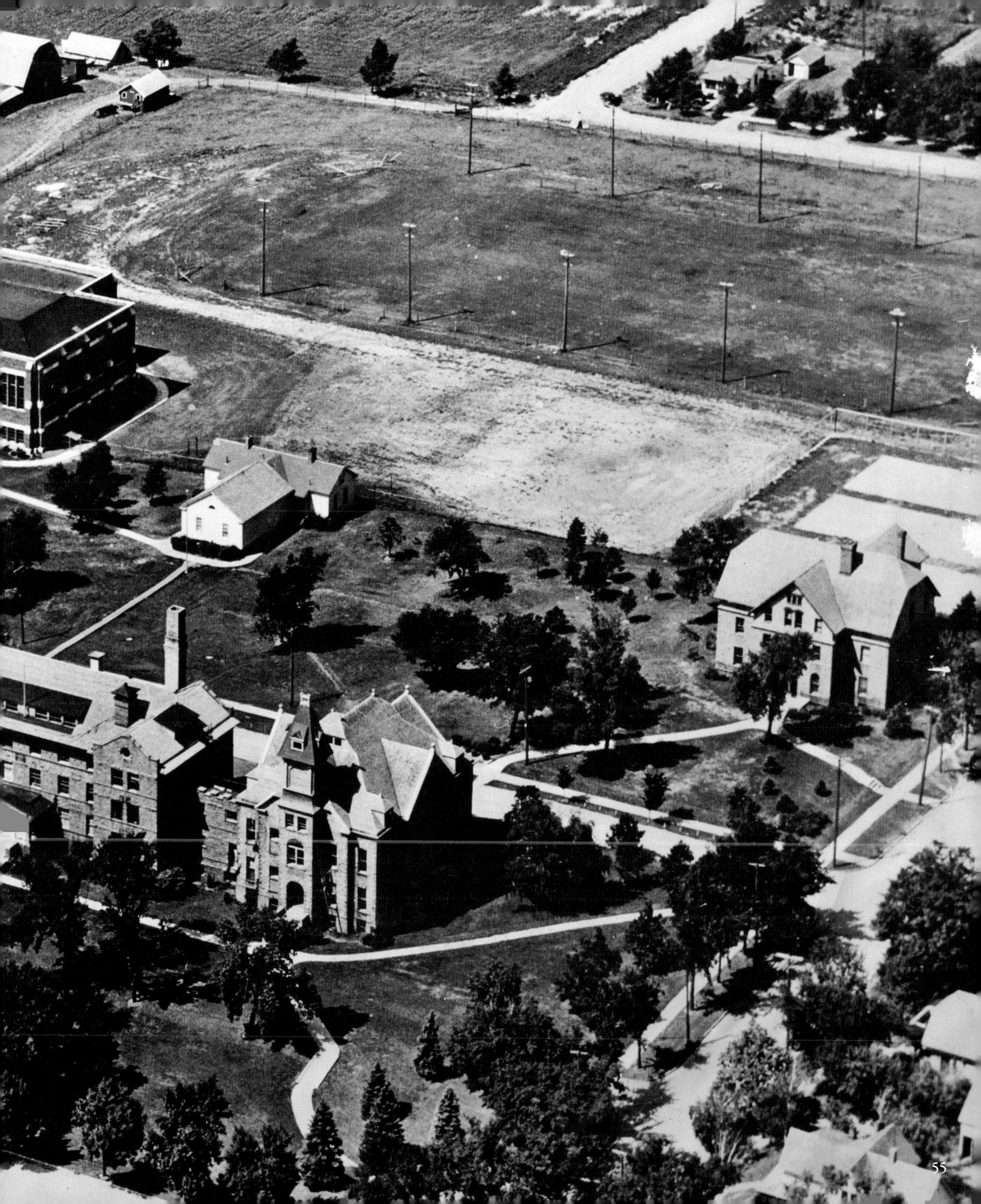

1939, Augustana 39, Mankato 0

ball!
AIN NIGHT
GUSTANA
K I N G S
25¢
TO ALL

Dr. John Froemke, professor of chemistry from 1930 to 1964

Augustana joins the North Central Conference.

The academic year opens with the largest enrollment in history, 587 students. By October 1, enrollment drops to 561; in the second semester of 1943, it is down to 410. On March 1, enrollment drops to 339. All of this is a result of the draft and enlistment of men into the military.

1942

Dr. V. R. Nelson (physics) and Dr. Sven Froiland (biology) join the faculty and make significant contributions to the natural sciences over the next four decades, helping to establish Augustana's preeminence in science education.

Barracks and a classroom building are moved from the Sioux Falls Air Base to house increasing postwar student population, classrooms, music studios, and science facilities.

1946

MEETING THE CHALLENGE 1940-1960

1941

Coach "Lefty" Olson leads the effort to build a new 2,800-seat Viking football stadium that ultimately costs $32,000. Much of the work and materials is donated.

1943

Due to World War II, the football program is suspended along with those at other North Central Conference schools.

1943-1965 The Rev. Dr. Lawrence Stavig is the fifteenth president. Prior to Augustana, he served as pastor of St. John Lutheran Church, Northfield, Minnesota.

Dr. Stavig develops a long-term plan; he outlines goals and operations of the College and a program for building facilities.

MEETING THE CHALLENGE 1940-1960

1950

Tuve Hall is dedicated.

1951

First Awards Day in May recognizes student scholarship.

1953

Augustana becomes the first Lutheran college to offer a four-year major in Education of the Deaf and Hard of Hearing.

Viking Varieties is held for the first time in the gym as part of Viking Days.

1950s-1960s

Campus organizations increase, including those for veterans studying under the GI Bill, social and honor societies, language, drama, and musical groups.

Augustana graduates are impressive scholars: Graduate scholarships received include Woodrow Wilson (14), Danforth (6), Fulbright (17), National Science (4), National Defense (22), Rockefeller (3), Rhodes (1).

1954

Pilot ground school courses are initiated.

1955

Mikkelsen Library is dedicated on September 15.

Solberg Hall is dedicated in October.

1957

Educational courses for credit are offered on television.

1958

First annual Augustana Band Festival is held February 7 and 8.

Paul Rogness '58 is second Rhodes Scholar.

1959

The football team is crowned North Central Conference champion.

Morrison Commons is dedicated on December 6.

Late 1950s

Faculty curriculum and policy committees are formed.

1960 STUDENT ENROLLMENT - 1,521 (1,177 full-time/344 part-time)

1940-1960

Meeting the Challenge

In 1940, World War II in Europe hit home. The United States began to strengthen its armed forces. Men of military age were required to register for the draft. Their educational plans put on hold, the number of students in colleges and universities decreased by nearly 50 percent. While educational institutions struggled to avoid closing their doors, many, including Augustana, managed to stay afloat with government training programs—such as aviation and nursing—to meet the demands of the crisis. In addition, President Granskou's team responded by reducing other courses and faculty where possible without jeopardizing the College's academic program. Granskou ably guided Augustana through an economy impacted by the nation's worst depression, decimating forces of nature in the heartland, and wartime until he was called to the presidency of St. Olaf College in 1943.

It was a new day when Lawrence Stavig arrived to lead the College in October of 1943. His pastoral ministry and distinguished service to the Church, as well as his ecumenical worldviews, brought broad experience to the presidency. His abilities were put to the test early on as he faced problems of fluctuating enrollment and lack of funds. In his first year, student numbers were down by nearly 200 from the previous year. With the shortfall in tuition and fees, once again the faculty was reduced—this time by one-third. Continual fluctuation in enrollments was the norm in the early 1940s, the effects of which were enough to try the patience of the best administrator.

At his inauguration, Dr. Stavig had announced an ambitious development plan for Augustana College to assess its goals and operation, including a three-phase building program—a total of nine buildings to be completed over a 25-year period. Internal expansion of the College was to occur simultaneously. Stavig held that a strong faculty, quality academics, and first-rate facilities were essential for educational excellence, and would be accomplished by increasing faculty salaries and student scholarships and strengthening ties with the Church, community, and the Augustana College Association.

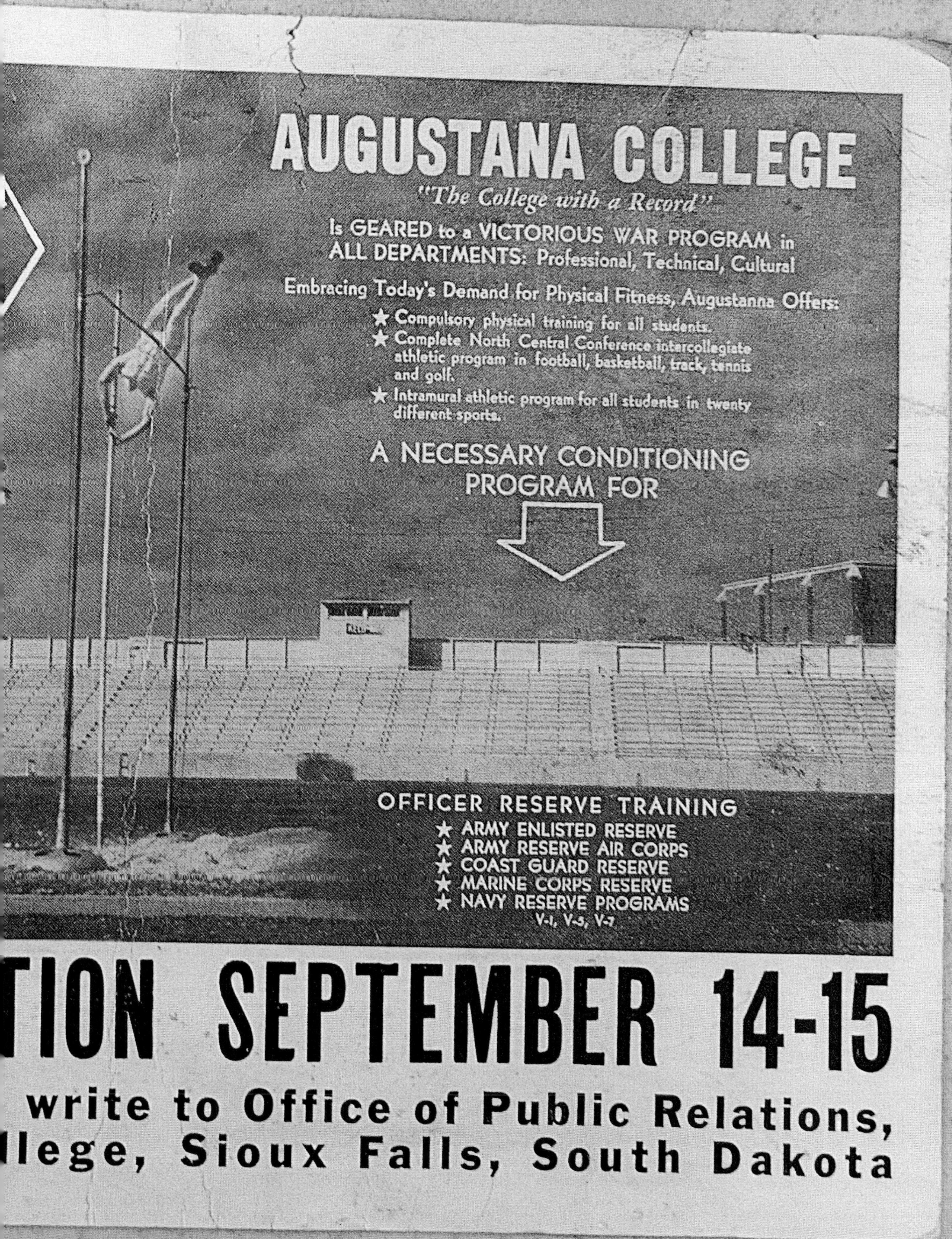

ca. 1940s, Officer training poster

e Augustana

MIRROR

Augustana College, Sioux Falls, S. Dak.

Vol. XVII, N

BEAT WASHBURN!

Enrollment Reaches All-Time Hig

necoming Set October 11-13

lization that Homecoming is short two weeks away was nly impressed upon the stu- last Monday, September 22, upperclassmen lined up be- the balloting boxes to vote ndidates for the 1946 Viking Queen, who will reign over ecoming on October 11-13.

pulation of the voting showed even senior girls were chosen eir fellow students to vie for title of queen. The second ion will be held soon.

ndidates for queen are Lois on, Sisseton; Doris Shay, Mt. non; Shirley Carls, Hartford; yll Mortensen, Gary; Elda Brookings; Elaine Brekke, e City, and Bernice Klinkel s, Canistota.

hairman of Viking Day is Bob dridge, senior. He announces former Augustana dean and cher, Dr. Martin L. Cole, now n at St. Olaf college, will ak at the alumni banquet. Dr. l O. Pederson, '27 Augustana duate and Lutheran pastor at

Registration day found veterans standing in line in the gym for their G. I. Bill information.

Latest Tabulatio Shows Total of 922 Students

After three days of regist Augustana's enrollment soa history-making proportions. all-time high of 922 stude over three times the numbe had registered here a year

This large enrollment is up of 501 ex-G.I. Joe's and who are taking advantage o Uncle Sam's generosity. I that the men are more av the necessity of higher ed than women because only the veterans are girls Veterans Administration h isdiction over all of these s

The remaining 421 s came to Augustana thro normal channels of enr This group is divided i women and 127 men.

It looks like a good the fairer sex in the soci for the ratio is more tha

Zabawa to Appear On Season's First Artist Program

Social Board Plans Annual Reception

Faculty members and students are invited to the annual re-

Ca. 1940s, Freshman Registration

Despite the war, or perhaps because of it, agriculture in the region was rallying and becoming increasingly more prosperous. The American economy as a whole also was improving. Society and the value system were changing as were opportunities for education, jobs, and lifestyles. People were seeking better wages, women were moving into the workforce, minorities were becoming more visible. Global issues were part of the national dialogue. International tension, heightened by the advent of nuclear weapons in countries other than the United States, the looming Korean War, and the Cuban Missile Crisis brought education under close government scrutiny with attempts to curb the scope of academics. Suddenly, critics believed there were too many frills in education. America lacked missiles and satellites. Science and math courses were to be enhanced. Augustana was not left untouched by all of this, but it was accustomed to adjusting, to doing whatever was necessary to stay the course set by those having gone before.

President Stavig had a stabilizing influence. As the nation and its educational institutions emerged during the postwar period, he and his staff prepared to accommodate returning veterans and the influx of postwar students—more mature, highly motivated, and supported by government aid programs such as the GI Bill. Enrollment skyrocketed in 1946. Major adjustments had to be made for housing and scheduling, with laboratories and classrooms filled beyond capacity. Barracks were moved to campus from the Sioux Falls Air Base and provided much-needed space for men's dormitories and a cafeteria. Additional government barracks were obtained to house music programs and the natural sciences. Student numbers began to even out, until the Korean War called men into service in 1950. Once again, the College had to adjust its budget when men exited for the armed services. However, Dr. Stavig was very good at keeping finances in check; the College rarely operated in the red on his watch.

1954, Groundbreaking for the Mikkelsen Library

Following the Korean conflict, colleges and universities experienced less fluctuation in enrollment and began planning ahead when it was projected that numbers of students would be on the rise. From 1950 to 1960, the Augustana campus was physically transformed with the completion of four new buildings—dormitories Tuve Hall and Solberg Hall, Mikkelsen Library, and the Morrison Commons, which housed dining facilities, a post office, bookstore, health center, and recreational and lounge rooms.

By the end of the decade, and into the next, students had nearly doubled in number and foreign students had increased as well. Graduates were garnering their share of prestigious scholarships such as the Woodrow Wilson, Danforth, Fulbright, and Rhodes, a result of Augustana's move toward more discerning admission policies and the increasing quality of the faculty and academic programs.

President Stavig was on course with the plan announced at his inauguration. In addition to new facilities, he also was encouraging faculty growth and doctorates for those who did not have them. In turn, the faculty now wanted input into shaping policy relative to tenure, advancement, salaries, leaves of absence, and curricula in order to maintain a good balance of the liberal arts and professional programs. In the 1950s, general education courses were restructured, religion courses were made consistent with those of other colleges of the Church, and a nursing major was developed. Augustana became a front-runner when it was the first Lutheran college to offer a major in Education of the Deaf and Hard of Hearing in affiliation with the South Dakota School for the Deaf. A pilot ground school course was initiated and there was a venture into educational television.

Student activities during the Stavig years reflected the times. In the patriotic war years, students grew accustomed to rationing and going without. In years of normalcy, there were the usual social and political organizations, service clubs, honor societies citing leadership and academics, and groups that continued to nurture the cultures of their native countries. Theatre and music were popular. The religion emphasis remained strong. Dr. Stavig served as chaplain for a number of years and discussions were initiated toward organizing a student congregation. Capping the decade of the '50s, the football team earned a North Central Conference championship in 1959 under colorful coach, Bob Burns.

1940s, Gymnasium – Chapel – Auditorium

1941, Viking home games

ca. 1947, Faculty and students at a special dinner in the basement of East Hall

AUGL
FLYIN

1948, The Augustana Flying Club with Dr. V. R. Nelson, club advisor and professor of physics from 1946 to 1992 (lower right)

1949, All Nations Christmas

edelig Jul

1950s, Solberg Hall

1950s, Solberg Hall room

FIRST SHOVEL fu
in the Ladies hall g
monies Wednesday mor
Dean of Women, Miss H
at the left. Former bu
Gilbertson unearthed t
(above) in the colorful

Start Work On

The Augustana

MIRRO

FI
in the
monies
Dean of
at the l
Gilberts
(above)

November 17, 1947 Augustana College, Sioux Falls, S. Dak.

Two New Buildings To Be Constructed

1950s, Tuve Hall room

er Gives
Address
Program

in observance
as held during
sday morning,

ormer chaplain
w veteran's ad-
at Sioux Falls
the Armistice
hich he stated
something man
omething close
d.
d that we can
d's way and we
peace until "we
ide of Jesus

Archi
Plan f
Wome

Decision
struction
ings at A
made by
tors at a
Nov. 10,
nounceme
L. M. St
being con
mediately
specificati
tion of a
and a libr

of Sioux Falls, made the spades look like teaspoons as the huge power shovel began to move dirt immediately following the formal ground-breaking ceremony. What started out as a mere scratching of the earth's surface soon developed into a seven foot hole over 100 feet long after four days of excavating. A huge crowd was in attendance at the opening day, and onlookers continued to watch the dramatic changes in the campus take place throughout the week. Construction of the $400,000 project will be completed by the fall of 1950 according to the contract.

ed over
cere-
ped by
ictured
G. H.
de-full
gram.

ew Ladies Hall

Dr. Glenn Sets Stage For Ground Breaking Ceremonies of $400,000 Job

By Laurel Gray

"Put off thy shoes from off thy feet, for the place whereon thou standest is holy ground:" (Exodus 3:5) With these words

1950s, Tuve Hall front desk

1951, Students guard the Viking Days bonfire site

1953, The first Viking Varieties

Split
Hares!

Saturday, October 10, 1953

AUGUST

Viking Days
Worshippers
Hear Hoyer

AUGUSTANA

Mirror

Augustana College, SIOUX FALLS, S. D.

NA CELEBRATES 30TH HOM

iking Varieties" ludes Best of llege Talent

dent, faculty and alumni will be combined tonight e **Viking Varieties** show uled for 8:14½ in the gym- n.

three — student, faculty lumni — will be combined emcees, Clara Chilson and Sather. The two will keep inety-minute show moving y.

student band, organized directed by Earl Colgan, ring up the curtain on show.

1 Schneider and Verona ss will combine alumni and talent with a piano duo. faculty members to parti- are Cliff Olson and Richard yahn.

e of the frosh talent dis- d at the orientation week show will be presented at ogram, too. Solveig Steen oxanne Kohrs will each

1953 Viking Days Queen

1957, Chapel in the Gymnasium – Chapel – Auditorium

1958, A 21–20 Viking Days victory over
St. Norbert College at Howard Wood Field

1959, Former First Lady Eleanor Roosevelt visits campus in January as part of the American Association for the United Nations tour

1952, Senator Richard Nixon greeting
the Augustana Choir in Washington, D.C.

1959, Band tour with concerts in Colorado, North Dakota, and South Dakota

1965-1980 Dr. Charles Balcer serves as the College's sixteenth president. He came to Augustana from St. Cloud State University where he was dean of academic administration.

1960

The Augustana Choir takes its first international tour to Norway and Germany as part of the centennial year celebration.

1966

Dedication of Gilbert Science Center is November 19 with Nobel laureate, Willard Libby, as keynote speaker. Dr. Sven Froiland is pivotal to development of the center.

ADAPTING TO CHANGE 1960-1985

1962

Classroom space and offices are added to the Science building, which becomes the Social Science building in 1966 when Gilbert Science Center is dedicated.

1963

Social dancing on campus is approved in April.

Augustana Student Congregation is launched on November 3.

Bergsaker Hall, the first coed residence, is dedicated September 12.

1967

Jabberwock coffeehouse, a major student venture, opens.

Sculpture, *Ole the Viking*, designed by Peter Eide '66, is dedicated.

Humanities Center, providing space for languages, religion, education, and music, is dedicated September 14.

1971

Cleveland industrialist and Sioux Falls native, Thomas Fawick, presents the College with a bronze casting of Michelangelo's *Moses*.

1976

ADAPTING TO CHANGE 1960-1985

1970

Center for Western Studies is created. Dr. Herbert Krause is the first director.

A fund-raising benefit at the Sioux Falls Arena features Myron Floren '42 and the Lawrence Welk orchestra.

1977

Wrestling team finishes second in NCAA Division II national championships.

1969

The new chapel is dedicated on October 1. Daily chapel returns.

1981

Midwest Institute for International Studies opens to provide intensive English language programs for international students.

1982

The original Eide-Dalrymple Art Gallery is dedicated on October 7.

Radio station KAUR, operated by students, is upgraded with new equipment and operates 24/7.

1984

1985 STUDENT ENROLLMENT - 1,866 (1,427 full-time/368 part-time/71 graduate students)

1983

Radio and television personality, Art Linkletter, is the featured speaker at the Augustana Fellows 20th anniversary celebration.

1980-1986 Dr. Bill Nelsen is the College's seventeenth president. Dr. Nelsen came to Augustana from St. Olaf College where he was vice president and dean.

1960-1985

Adapting to Change

1960 marked the centennial of Augustana, plans for which had been in the works for several years. President Stavig had announced: "The observance of our centennial during the year, beginning in May of 1960, is in preparation. It will pay tribute to the pioneers and will express our gratitude to God for what has been. But mainly it will be intended to help us better understand our position in the world of today and to plan for the greatest possible effectiveness in the future."

That year, accompanied by Dr. and Mrs. Stavig, the Augustana Choir took its first international tour to Norway and Germany where it received high accolades. There were special campus events and guest lecturers, and service and alumni awards. The centennial year was also the launch pad for the Second Century Fund Appeal geared toward a 15-year plan for major building and improvement projects, growing the endowment and scholarships, and continuing support for operations of the College. The drive was successful and helped eliminate debt on Solberg Hall and assisted in the construction of Morrison Commons.

Also, in 1960, the Evangelical Lutheran Church merged with two other synods to become the American Lutheran Church, which would provide direct financial support to Augustana and, more importantly, attract students to the College. Though support of the College by church constituencies had steadily increased in the past decade or so, actual budget contributions were now decreasing due to the expanded number of colleges, a result of the merger.

1960, The Augustana Choir, under the direction of Dr. Arnold Running, returns to Sioux Falls following its Centennial European Tour

The College set its sights on broadening its support base and advancing its influence. A director of alumni affairs was hired to establish relationships between the College and its alumni. A parents' association was formed to promote student recruitment and maintenance of high college standards, and Augustana Fellows focused on making the College a premier institution and increasing the endowment. All of this was very effective in moving the advancement goals of the College forward. And President Stavig, with his numerous associations on campus and beyond, was a visible and valuable presence.

Dr. Stavig was also continuing to focus on the long-range campus development plan he had announced nearly 20 years earlier. In 1962, classroom and office space was added to the Science building, which, at the time, consisted of renovated barracks. Bergsaker Hall, the first coed residence at Augustana, was dedicated in 1963, and ground was broken in 1965 for a new science building. Known as Gilbert Science Center, it was heralded at the time as one of the finest natural science facilities in the north-central United States.

Dr. Stavig stood firm in his vision and purpose of Christian higher education. The College and the Church bond continued to remain strong under his leadership. The Lutheran student body stayed constant and spiritual vitality was evidenced by daily chapel attendance. In their 20-plus years at Augustana, Dr. and Mrs. Stavig looked upon students, faculty, and alumni as family. Cora Stavig was clearly an asset to her husband's presidency as they entertained, counseled, and nurtured faculty and students.

1963, Board of Regents allows social dancing on campus

"The Sixties," as the decade of counterculture and social revolution was known, hosted a plethora of change—technological, social, economic, and political. Great strides were made in space exploration and man reached the moon. The Civil Rights Bill became law. A horrified nation watched as leaders were assassinated—President John Kennedy, and later Dr. Martin Luther King Jr. and Robert Kennedy, all of whom stood tall for civil rights. Women lobbied for equal employment and equal pay. Pollution and its effect on the planet came into question. There was the first heart transplant, and the laser was perfected. The *Sound of Music* was tops at the box office, the music of The Beatles flooded the airwaves, and young and old alike were dancing to Chubby Checker's "Twist." The world's first domed stadium was built, and the first Super Bowl game was played. The longtime conflict in Vietnam, with a half million U.S. troops in that country, cast a dark pall over the economy, politics, and social programs.

All of this and more, in one way or another, affected values, lifestyles, society—*and* education. The 800,000-plus World War II babies who entered college in the '60s were revolutionary in their thinking and birthed an activist movement. Theirs was a hippie culture, one of long hair, army fatigues, and peace signs. Students rallied for civil rights and against the war in Vietnam, and on their campuses they spoke out against such things as rules they believed to infringe on their personal lives and courses thought to be a waste in preparing for their futures. Their voices were indeed heard. Coed dorms came into existence, and experimental courses and new grading systems were instituted. Global links were now an integral part of doing business and students wanted a voice in academia and its role in shaping their futures.

Their voices were heard on campus social scenes as well. At Augustana, students questioned the longtime policy of no social dancing. Other colleges of the Church were beginning to allow it and parents were raising no real objection so, after several years of deliberation by school officials, the first dance at Augustana was held in the fall of 1963. In the words of Dr. Sandra Looney, professor of English: "The first dance on campus I remember well because I was a chaperone—my husband and I. The strange thing . . . It was in the gym and the students just could not bring themselves to dance. Somehow they couldn't break the barrier, so the faculty danced, the chaperones danced, and the students sort of stood on the outside, very hesitant to get in [involved]."

When Dr. Charles Balcer came to the presidency of the College, faculty and campus growth, curriculum development, and capital assets were staying the course. Dr. Balcer was inaugurated as the 16th and first lay president of Augustana in September of 1965. Though not a churchman *per se*, he had amassed a wealth of educational experience. In addition to continuing on the ambitious development path laid out by President Stavig, the new president had plans of his own—to further strengthen the College's academic reputation with attention to faculty and program development, and to build relationships with area congregations of the American Lutheran Church. Doing so, Balcer believed, would help create a clearer understanding of the role of the Church in supporting its colleges. He was a proponent of the College and the wider community working together, emphasizing the benefits each could bring to the other. And, he wanted Augustana to become a more formidable force in athletics.

The late '60s, and into the next decade, were crucial years in the history of the College and the nation. At Augustana, student restlessness was mild compared to many other schools, but rally groups did take root. The students pressed for attention to human rights—recruitment of minority students and faculty, and curriculum that emphasized contributions of black and American Indian students. Awareness of the plight of the American Indians was heightened in 1969 when a group orchestrated a lock-in at Bergsaker Hall in protest of a Lutheran Indian ministry they felt had not lived up to expectations. The war in Vietnam and its draft were cause for anxiety, especially as it wore on and President Balcer promoted an ROTC program—which never materialized due to mixed views of the campus constituency. Most believed that a military training program was not appropriate for a church college.

A handbook was developed that laid out rights and responsibilities of students. New policies were implemented relative to campus life. Students gained representation on faculty committees, dormitory visitation policies and women's dorm hours were changed, and, though a controversial topic to this day, smoking was permitted. Honor societies survived this turbulent period but a number of student societies did not. Religious participation on campus varied in intensity and commitment, too. But customs such as Viking Days and celebrations of Christmas were a constant. Though the students were assertive, they were also entrepreneurial—the Jabberwock coffeehouse, a major student endeavor, opened in 1967.

Full-time and part-time student enrollment was increasing which, as always, required attention to increasing the faculty. That necessitated the addition of administrative and support personnel. Consequently, the operations umbrella was expanding. Dr. Balcer developed a more efficient administrative strategy, perhaps a result of his military service. It was one of delegated responsibility, with vice presidents appointed in such areas as academic, financial, and student affairs who, in turn, reported to him.

In the early '70s, a Curriculum Study Committee made recommendations for change. Recognizing that Augustana should remain a strong liberal arts college, it reaffirmed its relationship to the Church and pledged to be faithful to the Christian tradition. However, the College would be free to examine both religious and secular values. The 4-1-4 academic calendar would now consist of two semesters and a January term. A core of general education studies, to be required of all students, was outlined. The bachelor of science degree was dropped with only the bachelor of arts degree to be awarded to those completing undergraduate studies. The calendar change gave way to new opportunities for learning, such as internships, study abroad, and on-campus multicultural studies.

During these years, there was great opportunity for faculty professional growth, and classroom and laboratory experiences were enhanced with grants from the National Science Foundation and the National Endowment for the Humanities.

Throughout Balcer's presidency, funding for operations was always in a state of flux. Though enrollments were up, an inflated economy and fewer available federal government dollars were thorns in the College budget. Church contributions did not always keep pace, and the College was attempting to keep tuition increases at a minimum.

Not all things during these years, however, were doom and gloom. Several fund-raising campaigns helped to move Augustana forward. The College received capital expansion dollars from the Church, and successful college drives resulted in financial support for programming, ongoing faculty professional growth, scholarships, and for the renovation of Old Main and construction of the Humanities building. Two new residence halls, identical eight-story towers eventually named for Clemens M. Granskou and Lawrence M. Stavig, claimed their places on the campus in 1969. An all-weather track, married student housing, and a maintenance center were constructed, and renovations on East Hall and the Administration building were undertaken, both of which are now listed on the National Register of Historic Places.

In 1979, construction began on an addition to the Mikkelsen Library and groundbreaking for a new chapel occurred in the spring of 1980. The Augustana Student Congregation had become a recognized member congregation of the American Lutheran Church. Notable musical programs were thriving, and Dr. Balcer's goal to accelerate and improve the competitive edge of Augustana athletics was being attained. Focused recruiting efforts ultimately resulted in successes in football, basketball, wrestling, and women's intercollegiate athletics.

ca. 1970, Ogden Dalrymple, professor of art from 1946 to 1991

1970, "Pastor Pete" Petersen Leads worship

An important part of the mission of Augustana has been to serve the people of the northern Great Plains. Created in 1970, the Center for Western Studies documents early contact with indigenous peoples and exploration and resettlement by European Americans. Through its archives, library, and publications, it preserves and interprets the history and cultures of the Great Plains region of the American West and provides a cultural context not only for Augustana, but for other educational organizations and the community at large. The College also collaborates with several educational institutions in and around Sioux Falls who provide basic skills training, continuing education courses, and ecumenical theological education for clergy and laity.

From student unrest to social turbulence, Balcer's administration weathered a number of storms; yet, none were as emotionally charged or spiritually challenging as the 1969 plane crash that claimed six lives from Augustana—Frayne Anderson, the librarian; K. Don Tibbetts, the debate coach; and students Joyce Estwick, Linda Heidemann, Alan Jensen, and James Houske, all of whom were returning from a debate tournament in Colorado Springs.

The Piper Cherokee disappeared the evening of January 11 following the pilot's last radio contact with an air controller at North Platte, Nebraska. The next day, a massive search effort began with volunteers combing wide areas of Nebraska and South Dakota. Three days later, a convoy of cars carried nearly 200 Augustana students and faculty to Sioux City, Iowa, to participate in a ground search. The search continued until January 25 when it was suspended due to harsh cold. Augustana, however, was not about to give up. President Balcer sent letters to some 25,000 farmers in the area where the plane was presumed to have gone down, asking them to search their property. On March 25, the wreckage was found 12 miles west of Anselmo, Nebraska. A memorial service was held in the gymnasium chapel to mourn the victims with "Pastor Pete" Petersen officiating.

Charles Balcer vacated the presidency in July 1980, leaving a legacy of growth—in enrollment, faculty and staff, physical plant, and programs for serving the Church and the area. The College had more graduates during Balcer's 14-year presidency than it had in the preceding 105 years. After a leave, he returned to Augustana in 1981 as distinguished professor of speech, drama, and communication.

When Augustana welcomed Dr. Bill Nelsen as its president in 1980, the nation also had a new president whose operative word was conservatism. The economic plan of America's president shaped government policies that affected many educational institutions. There was a reduction in student financial aid and a domino effect was felt when aid to state schools was diminished and private colleges realized they had competition for funds from the private sector's foundations, corporations, and individuals. Dr. Nelsen prepared to deal with reduced government spending and also declining enrollment due, in part, to a marked decrease in numbers of high school graduates and increased tuition and fees necessary to compensate for the inflation fallout of the late '70s.

There are always challenges for colleges and universities, and those of the 1980s were no exception at Augustana. Factor in that the College is located in the heartland of agriculture, which is always affected by the farm economy, and the financial picture can be predictable.

President Nelsen was up to the challenge. His education covered a broad spectrum. His doctorate was in political science, and he had studied philosophy and theology in Germany as a Fulbright Scholar. He was comfortable in academia, having served as vice president and dean at St. Olaf College prior to coming to Augustana. Early on, he outlined a "Challenge and Renewal Program" for the College to review and rethink its mission and goals as a college of the Church. He made faculty and personnel adjustments as needed and created a provost position for a more coordinated program of services to students. Although the new Augustana chapel was dedicated on October 1, 1981, fund-raising was difficult. At one point, Dr. Nelsen declared that the interior would not be completed until necessary funds were in hand. Eventually, cost of the $857,500 facility was completely funded by contributions. With the encouragement of Dr. Nelsen, the College returned to a schedule of daily chapel worship. Student ministry outreach teams were active and the campus congregation was involved in the settlement of refugees.

New initiatives included an intensive English language program for international students, on-the-job and independent study experiences, tutoring, mentoring, and career planning. Augustana musicians were continuing to move toward national and international recognition. Theatre productions were of the more modern, and, in 1983, the debate team claimed a significant presence nationally. Women's tennis and softball teams won North Central Conference championships. The wrestling team achieved national recognition and track and field star, Jeff Gross '85, qualified for the Olympic trials in 1984 with record-breaking performances in the 400-meter dash. And, in 1985, the first professional public radio station, KRSD, began to operate on campus.

In 1985, to continue the mission and goals as a college of the Church announced early in his presidency, Dr. Nelsen put the Commitment to Excellence campaign into motion. Mary Harum Hart '72, cohost of television's "Entertainment Tonight," served as emcee at the kickoff event. Centerpiece of the $6 million-plus campaign was the construction of a health and physical education facility, now known as Elmen Center, and a goal to meet endowment challenge grants offered by the National Endowment for the Humanities and Lutheran Brotherhood [now Thrivent Financial for Lutherans].

1980, College chapel construction

1981, College chapel

1960, Viking Days royalty

1960, "The Far-off Hills," directed by Earl Mundt, professor of theatre from 1950 to 1981

VIKING DAYS
OCT. 12
1963
SIOUX FALLS, S.D.
DRUGS
CLEANERS
EASTWOLD
Walgreens
DRUGS
VIKING DAYS

1961, Viking Days parade

1963–1964, Cheerleaders

DAGE

1964, Dr. Don Fryxell, professor of English from 1953 to 1980, teaches classes on KELO Television

1965, Bowling alley in Morrison Commons, now known as The Back Alley

1969, Augustana at the G.E. College Bowl, Rockefeller Center, New York City

SCHRADER
LEW NADY
COLLEGE

1970, THE WEBS

WEBS

1971, Marching Band, directed by Dr. Leland Lillehaug, professor of music from 1956 to 1992

1972, Cheerleaders

1973, Brass Choir, directed by Dr. Harold "Doc" Krueger, professor of music from 1965 to 1994

1972, Viking Days Central Committee

VIKING DAYS '72
OCT. 26-29
AUGIE
AUGUSTANA COLLEGE

1975, Class of 1979 at freshman orientation

A
AUGUSTANA COLLEGE

1977-1978, North Central Conference Champions, coached by Mel Klein and John Thomas

VIKINGS
52
VIKINGS
42
VIKINGS
40
VIKINGS
12
VIKINGS
20
VIKINGS
14
VIKINGS
50

SOLBERG
STAVIG

ca. 1977, Augustana Student Association elections

A NEW ERA 1985-2000

1985

The 125th anniversary of the College is celebrated during the 1985-1986 academic year.

Commitment to Excellence to advance the mission of the College is launched with Mary Harum Hart '72 from "Entertainment Tonight" serving as emcee. Centerpiece of the $6.35 million campaign is construction of a health and physical education facility, and to meet endowment challenge grants.

1986

The 125th anniversary sculpture commissioned by the College, "Hindsight, Insight, Foresight" (The Owls), crafted by art professors, Ogden Dalrymple and Palmer Eide, is dedicated in April.

The Augustana Plan, a new curriculum for the College, is implemented.

Dr. Henry Kissinger, former U. S. Secretary of State, lectures on campus at the first Van Demark Lecture in October.

1986-1987 The Rev. Dr. Sidney Rand, former president of St. Olaf College and former U.S ambassador to Norway, is appointed interim president.

1987

The freshman class is the last to wear beanies.

1987-1992 The Rev. Dr. Lloyd Svendsbye, the nineteenth president, begins his term of office on June 1.

Groundbreaking is held on July 13 for the health, physical education, and recreation facility. Brothers Robert and James Elmen contribute a $1 million naming gift.

Dr. Richard Leakey, noted paleoanthropologist, and Dr. Stephen Jay Gould, evolutionary theorist from Harvard University, are Van Demark Lecture speakers in November.

1988

Erling and Clara Haugo provide $1 million for endowed scholarships.

In his fourth year as head football coach, Jim Heinitz is recognized as the 1988 Kodak College Coach of the Year in Region 4. The Vikings finish 8-3 and qualify for their first-ever NCAA Division II playoffs.

1989

The Elmen Center is dedicated.

Arthur Miller, at the time America's preeminent living playwright, speaks at the Van Demark Lecture on March 28.

The Chapel of Reconciliation is formally named by the Board of Regents at its spring meeting.

The bowling alley in Morrison Commons is removed and the entire renovated space is renamed The Back Alley.

1990

The original Model School building, which was converted to the Central Services operation on campus, is demolished on November 6.

Ellen Goodman, Pulitzer Prize winner, is the featured speaker at the Augustana Fellows dinner on May 3.

Nobel Peace Prize laureate, Elie Wiesel, is the Van Demark Lecture speaker on April 30.

1991

Augustana becomes the third Internet provider in South Dakota [after the University of South Dakota and Earth Resources Observation and Science (EROS) Center] and, subsequently, provides Internet access for other state universities.

Edward and Edith Mortenson '41 Delman contribute $1 million for "an education center for theatre and fine arts."

Augustana softball team, coached by Dr. Sandy Jerstad, wins the NCAA Division II national championship, the first in College history.

1992

President Lloyd Svendsbye resigns from the presidency on March 30. The Rev. Dr. Sidney Rand is named interim president for the second time.

Nobel laureate, Elie Wiesel, and former U.S. Vice President Walter Mondale speak at the Nobel Peace Prize Forum on campus.

1993-2000 Dr. Ralph Wagoner becomes the twenty-first president of Augustana.

William F. Buckley, nationally syndicated columnist, speaks at the Van Demark Lecture in April.

1993

Former Soviet president, Mikhail Gorbachev, speaks at the third Boe Forum on Public Affairs.

1996

A NEW ERA 1985-2000

1994

The first Community Service Day is held on May 4.

Augustana is in the "Top Ten" regional liberal arts colleges named in *U.S. News & World Report*.

The Augustana Choir, under the direction of Dr. James Johnson, performs in France in June to commemorate the 50th anniversary of the Allied invasion and liberation of Europe.

1995

Augustana Renewal, a $31 million campaign, the most ambitious fund-raising campaign to date, is launched in January. Primary capital project is to build a new social science center.

The Center for Western Studies announces the largest gift to the College at the time from former governor of South Dakota, Nils A. Boe, and his sisters, Borghild Boe '30 and Lois Boe Hyslop '35. The first Boe Forum on Public Affairs is held in March with General Colin Powell. Later that year, the second Boe Forum features former President George H. W. Bush.

Women's cross-country is ranked sixth in the nation.

The Board of Regents adopts a set of core values—Christian, Liberal Arts, Excellence, Community and Service—that becomes the foundation for the College's academic and student life programs.

John Major, former prime minister of the United Kingdom, and former First Lady Barbara Bush, speak at the Boe Forum on Public Affairs.

Emeriti professors, Drs. Joyce and V. R. Nelson, provide a gift, the first ever in the history of the College given by former faculty members, to build the Nelson Service Center.

1998

2000 STUDENT ENROLLMENT - 1,783 (1,623 full-time/105 part-time/55 graduate students)

1997

Terry Waite, at the time an adviser to the Archbishop of Canterbury and who had endured four years as a hostage in Lebanon, speaks at the Nobel Peace Prize Forum on campus.

Lou and Helen Madsen make a multimillion-dollar gift to build a new Social Science building that will be called the Madsen Center.

1999

The Madsen Center is dedicated on October 1.

Nobel Peace Prize recipient, Archbishop Desmond Tutu, addresses a crowd of 3,800 in the Elmen Center at the Boe Forum on Public Affairs.

The Augustana Band, under the direction of Dr. Bruce Ammann, is the first collegiate band to perform in the demilitarized zone dividing the Koreas.

1986, "HINDSIGHT, INSIGHT, FORESIGHT" (THE OWLS) DE

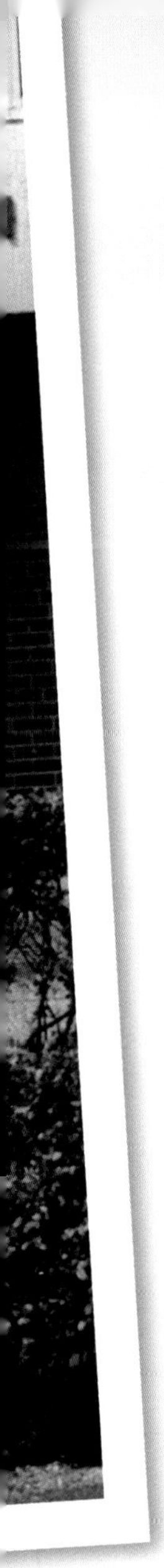

1985-2000
A New Era

Throughout its proud history, Augustana experienced diverse changes and varied areas of emphasis, as well as secular challenges, but its mission remained clear—to provide an academically rigorous liberal arts education within a Christian context. In its very infancy, when the primary purpose was to prepare men for the ministry, the liberal arts were part of the theological curriculum. The College weathered economic and financial trials, societal changes, transformation within the Church, and a myriad of issues and needs on behalf of students and staff. The 1980s and 1990s were no different.

The world was on a fast track. The development of technology was escalating and people's lives were changing more quickly than they had in the past due, in part, to global participation with new, industrialized economies and the collapse of communism. Enter Nintendo, use of home computers, and sport utility vehicles. Within months of each other in 1986, the U.S. space program suffered a setback when the Challenger disaster took seven lives, and the Chernobyl nuclear accident in Ukraine spewed radioactive debris into the atmosphere. First Lady Nancy Reagan, in her campaign to discourage drug use, was telling the nation to "just say no." In the United States, people marked the first national holiday to commemorate the birthday of Dr. Martin Luther King, Jr. In 1987, the Constitution of the United States was 200 years old and, in 1989, the world celebrated when the Berlin Wall came down. Credit cards and "designer" fashions were in. Family structures changed drastically during these years with more divorces and, consequently, more single parent families. Two wage-earners per family were more common than in previous decades, as more women chose to earn college and advanced degrees, marry, and have fewer children.

American education was experiencing emerging innovation. There was a call to return to the classics in colleges, and campuses across the country worked to get "back to the basics." After nearly 15 years, in 1985 the faculty of the College approved a new general education curriculum, the Augustana Plan, to be implemented during the 1986-1987 academic year. Considered a well-rounded plan, it was developed not only for a student's career, but for a student's life. It was organized to work well with the general education requirements, channel students into taking a broader background of general education courses, and to meet the needs and opportunities of other majors as well. The new curriculum included "bookends," a New Student Seminar for beginning freshmen and a Capstone course for seniors.

During the 1985-1986 academic year, Augustana celebrated 125 years, chronicled by Dr. Donald Sneen in *Through Trials and Triumphs: A History of Augustana College*. There were special events, including the dedication of the anniversary sculpture commissioned by the College, "Hindsight, Insight, Foresight," commonly referred to as "The Owls," crafted by iconic art professors, Ogden Dalrymple and Palmer Eide.

Jack Anderson, well-known investigative journalist, appeared at the spring 1986 Augustana Fellows dinner held at the Sioux Falls Convention Center. The first Van Demark Lecture in October featured Dr. Henry Kissinger, former U.S. Secretary of State. The lecture series, though held only a few years, was supported by grants from the Guy E. Van Demark Educational and Charitable Trust—Dr. Van Demark being South Dakota's first board certified orthopedic surgeon—and included other notable guests such as Dr. Richard Leakey, acclaimed paleoanthropologist; Dr. Stephen Jay Gould, evolutionary theorist from Harvard University; Arthur Miller, America's preeminent living playwright at the time; Elie Wiesel, Nobel Peace Prize winner and Holocaust survivor; and William F. Buckley, nationally syndicated columnist. Amid mixed emotions, historic Old Main was vacated and the windows boarded.

Dr. Nelsen resigned the presidency of the College in the summer of 1986 and later accepted the position of president and chief executive officer of Citizens' Scholarship Foundation of America in Saint Peter, Minnesota. He had capably managed Augustana's finances, increasing the endowment from $2 million to nearly $6 million. Capital debt had been reduced, the College budget was on track, and the challenge grants campaign was successfully launched.

CA. 1990, THE BACK ALLEY

While the search for a successor to President Nelsen was being conducted, The Rev. Dr. Sidney Rand, president emeritus of St. Olaf College and a former U.S. ambassador to Norway, was called out of retirement to serve as Augustana's interim president. His background included that of parish pastor, associate professor of religion at Concordia-Moorhead, and president of Waldorf College, Forest City, Iowa. He had also served as the first executive director of the American Lutheran Church Board of College Education. During Dr. Rand's presidency, Augustana began to recruit students from Norway.

Dr. Rand's brief tenure ended when The Rev. Dr. Lloyd Svendsbye was named president in June of 1987. Dr. Svendsbye had served as academic dean at St. Olaf College and president of Luther [Northwestern] Seminary. In his inaugural address on October 23, President Svendsbye said, "The liberal arts college . . . is duty bound to ask such questions as why, what for, on what basis? The liberal arts college must . . . continue to ask not only about truth and justice, but about the good and the beautiful. These questions must be asked in order that the liberal arts college may say a humanizing word in a culture moving quickly toward dehumanization."

Top of mind for Dr. Svendsbye, as it was for his predecessor, was the necessity to garner financial support for facilities, faculty salaries, scholarships, payment of debt, and for other needs. All one had to do was read his commentaries in the *Augustana Today*, the publication for alumni and friends of the College, to realize how significant a challenge he faced and how preoccupied he was with this task. Shortly after President Svendsbye arrived at Augustana, one of the first exciting events on the campus was the July 13 groundbreaking for the health, physical education, and recreation facility for which brothers, Robert '52 and James '60 Elmen, had contributed a $1 million naming gift.

On January 1, 1988, sharing common beliefs and mission, and a rich and diverse heritage, the American Lutheran Church, the Lutheran Church in America, and the Association of Evangelical Lutheran Churches merged to become the Evangelical Lutheran Church in America, making it the largest Lutheran denomination in the country.

The College was experiencing record enrollment of part-time students; Norwegian was being taught, reviving the College's interest in its heritage; and a gift of $1 million was received from Erling and Clara Haugo for endowed scholarships. To round things out, in 1988 the Vikings qualified for their first-ever NCAA Division II football playoffs.

The Nobel Peace Prize Forum, an annual conference held with the blessing of the Norwegian Nobel Institute in Oslo, was founded in 1989 by Dr. Rand and former U. S. Vice President Walter Mondale. The event gives recognition to Norway's international peace efforts and offers opportunities for Nobel Peace Prize laureates, diplomats, scholars, and the general public to share in dialogue on the dynamics of peacemaking and the underlying causes of conflict and war. The first forum was held at St. Olaf College. Subsequent forums have rotated among the campuses of five Midwestern colleges of the Evangelical Lutheran Church in America, all founded by Norwegian immigrants—Augustana, Augsburg, Concordia-Moorhead, Luther, and St. Olaf.

In 1988, the Elmen Center opened and the Chapel of Reconciliation was formally named by the Board of Regents in 1989. The bowling alley in Morrison Commons was removed and the entire space was renovated and renamed The Back Alley, a location for coffeehouse discussions, dances, and other student activities. Green: The Environmental Committee, a student environmental group, began an ongoing campus-wide recycling effort.

Technology took a giant leap in the 1990s. The World Wide Web forever changed how we communicate, how we spend our money, and how the world does business. Online educational opportunities were offered—no longer did you have to *come* to school to *go* to school. Construction was begun on the International Space Station. Dolly the sheep was cloned, the Human Genome Project was initiated, and the application of DNA was expanded. No one needed to ask for directions as the global positioning system became operational. Biodegradable products and genetically engineered crops were developed. Cell phones were becoming more prevalent—though fairly cumbersome, not yet the sleek, pocket-sized, must-have versions of today.

President Svendsbye was, as always, keeping an eye on finances while steering Augustana toward keeping pace with the rapidly expanding global economy. Signs were evident on campus when the Soviet National Team of Ukraine came to play the Vikings in basketball, and Augustana became the third Internet provider in the state of South Dakota, subsequently providing Internet access for other state universities.

In late 1990, the Central Services building was razed. The building had been constructed as the Model School in 1911, which was an addition to the original school hospital built in 1910. A $1 million gift from Edward and Edith Mortenson '41 Delman was received in 1991 and designated for an educational center for theatre and fine arts. Edith Mortenson had been in charge of the business office of the College from 1941 to 1945, and had also served on the Board of Regents.

On March 30, 1992, President Lloyd Svendsbye resigned his office. Dr. Sidney Rand once again stepped into the role of interim president until it was announced in February 1993 that Dr. Ralph Wagoner from Western Illinois University had been unanimously elected president of the College. Wagoner said, "My family's Lutheran background and the academic stature of Augustana were major influences in my decision to pursue the president's position. This is a class institution, and I hope you all realize how truly, truly honored I am to be here."

Wagoner took the helm in September. He came to the College confronted with what Interim President Rand described in his last commentary in the *Augustana Today* as "a restlessness and degree of unhappiness among our personnel." Rand concluded, speaking of Wagoner, "I can say that Augustana is fortunate and all of us look forward to a lively and provocative time in the life of the College." Upon learning of Wagoner's resignation as president of Western Illinois to accept the presidency of Augustana, Illinois Governor Jim Edgar wrote to him, "It was with mixed emotions that I learned Augustana of South Dakota had the wisdom to offer you its presidency. You have been an outstanding university president."

In his inaugural address, Wagoner said, "Augie must be a player, not a spectator. Augie must appreciate, nurture, and carry its fair share of the load if we are to fulfill our responsibility. Augie must stand side by side with our partners. Augustana College must seize those opportunities that are consistent with our mission, and by doing so benefit our students and faculty, our staff, our alumni, and our society." He closed his address with a saying that would conclude every formal remark he made on and off campus during his presidency: "It's a great day to be a Viking."

Ralph Wagoner was the right person for the times. He was chosen to "hit the ground running," and he did. He became known to the students simply as Ralph and loved to be in their presence. During occasional meals in the dining room, Dr. Wagoner could be seen with a tray, walking about serving up cookies while cracking jokes with the students. At the beginning of each academic year, at Christmastime for Wagoner Wonderland, and in between, Ralph and his wife, Susie, opened their home and their arms to the students.

The College hosted a number of fine presenters in the '90s. Among them were Elie Wiesel, Nobel Peace Prize laureate, who visited in 1992 for the Nobel Peace Prize Forum. The forum also hosted Terry Waite, hostage negotiator, in 1997; Pulitzer Prize winner Ellen Goodman; Betty Friedan, credited with launching the modern women's movement; and Garrison Keillor of "A Prairie Home Companion" and Minnesota Public Radio fame.

The Augustana Mirror, over the years, covered a plethora of campus news—sports, weekly highlights, course announcements, student views, and reminders of scholarship opportunities. During the '90s, according to archived issues of the *Mirror*, campus topics included students being shunned for expressing unconventional views, the pros and cons of abortion, and whether or not more low-fat, low-calorie meals should be offered. A sexual assault and harassment forum was held in 1995. An AIDS Awareness Week in March 1996 featured the nationally recognized AIDS quilt on campus. The Augustana Student Association ran a prominent story relative to its goals, which included residence hall improvements, student leadership opportunities, and student awareness of the association. The Augustana Choir, led by Dr. James Johnson, performed in France in 1994 to commemorate the 50th anniversary of the Allied invasion and liberation of Europe. Capstone classes came under fire by students who felt classes were too large, that they were not learning as they should.

1994, President Ralph Wagoner directs traffic on move-in day

KAUR, Augustana's radio station, continued to broadcast daily from Tuve Hall. Unlike any other station around, it was completely operated by students and community volunteers, and dealt with everything from government regulations and music companies to daily programming. In 1993, when the station faced complaints about questionable programming, one listener told the Board of Regents, "KAUR is the voice of Augustana College. More importantly, it's the voice of the students. It represents their lifestyle, their talents, and their creativity. It is a modern blend of humanities, business, and technology. There are few stations like it in the country: student run, with community and college together—a big voice on such a small budget." KAUR was permitted to continue on-air with the establishment of an advisory board. Today, KAUR is affiliated with Minnesota Public Radio providing day-to-day news and information programming, operations, and maintenance.

Augustana Renewal, up to this time, the most ambitious fund-raising campaign in the College's history, was launched in January 1995. Although comprehensive in nature, the primary capital project of the $31 million effort was to build a new social science center to replace the existing army barracks and completely renovate the Old Gym to include a new theatre to replace the "Little Theatre" in the Social Science building. A new corporate logo was developed to replace one that had been in use for 20 years. A number of students described the new graphic as "more up-to-date," "Ivy League-ish," "more dignified and academic, cool." CD-ROMs and databases became permanent in the Mikkelsen Library and were networked on campus.

In the same year, the Center for Western Studies announced the largest gift to the College at the time in the form of a trust from former South Dakota Governor Nils Boe and his sisters, Borghild Boe '30 and Lois Boe Hyslop '35. The purpose of the $2 million gift was "to bring to the College and the region a speaker who will address a topic of importance to the nation." Retired Gen. Colin Powell, former chairman of the U. S. Joint Chiefs of Staff, and former President George H. W. Bush were the first two speakers in the inaugural year for the Boe Forum on Public Affairs in 1995. Among other speakers in the late '90s were

1991, KAUR, Augustana's radio station

ca. 1990, Ceramics in Art Building 3

Mikhail Gorbachev, president of the Soviet Union, former British Prime Minister John Major, U.S. First Lady Barbara Bush, and Nobel Peace Prize laureate, Archbishop Desmond Tutu.

A faculty committee chaired by Dr. Arthur Olsen, Stanley L. Olsen Chair of Moral Values, adopted a set of five core values which were subsequently approved by the faculty and adopted by the Board of Regents in 1995. They serve as the foundation for the College's academic and student life programs:

Christian - As a college of the Church, we welcome all faiths, encourage spiritual growth, and relate Christian faith and ethics to learning and service.

Liberal Arts - Augustana provides an education of enduring worth by affirming that teaching and learning are central and lifelong; the breadth of our curriculum provides students with the skills and flexibility necessary for successful careers in a complex world.

Excellence - Committed to high standards and integrity.

Community - Augustana fosters an environment of participation, caring, respect, and empowerment.

Service - Affirming that wholeness includes reaching out to others.

A multimillion-dollar naming gift was received in 1997 from Lou and Helen Madsen to build a new Social Science building. The Madsens and two of their daughters, Vicki '80 and Pamela '83, were present for the groundbreaking on March 30, 1998. In May, an informal demolition ceremony for the removal of the Social Science building took place to make way for the ongoing construction of the Madsen Center with Dr. Lyn Oyos, professor emeritus of history, swinging the first sledgehammer.

That same year, Sally Fantle contributed $2 million to help fund two campus projects: $500,000 for the Madsen Center and a $1.5 million naming gift for a new Center for Western Studies. Central to the fund-raising efforts for the center, as well as the point person for the Boe Forum gift, was Dr. Art Huseboe, executive director of the center. In 1998, Emeriti professors, Drs. Joyce and V. R. Nelson, provided a gift, the first ever in the history of the College given by former faculty members, to build the Nelson Service Center.

A new model for student residential life came about in 1998 as the College approved the first purchase of a "theme house" that would eventually be named Valhalla. Over the next 10 years, the College's housing program took a major turn from the six traditional residence halls to the addition of 16 theme homes on the perimeter of the campus. The College also acquired two nearby apartment complexes, Duluth Place and the Schoeneman Apartments, and built the Summit Apartments at the corner of 33rd Street and Summit Avenue. Most recently, the College purchased the former Ronald McDonald House on Norton Avenue and renamed it the Global Education House.

At the end of the decade, the Augustana Band, led by Dr. Bruce Ammann, performed in the demilitarized zone dividing the Koreas, the first collegiate band to do so. The band was hosted by the U.S. military in Korea, and went on to perform concerts in Japan and China. In 1999, Old Main, officially abandoned in 1986, received a face-lift to protect the building. A new roof was added, the quartzite outer surface was tuck-pointed, and all windows were repaired and shuttered until such time as funds are available for the building's renovation. The new Madsen Center was dedicated on the first day of October. The Old Gym was completely renovated into a theatre and office complex for student services and was renamed the Edith Mortenson Center.

The decade was complete when Norwegian Crown Prince Haakon came to Augustana, his visit the first by a member of the Norwegian royal family since that of his grandparents in 1939, at the time Crown Prince Olav and Crown Princess Martha.

ca. 1985, Dr. Lynwood Oyos,
professor of history from 1957 to 1994

Hudson,
Dust

ca. 1985, Dr. Joyce Nelson, professor of nursing from 1967 to 1996

ca. early 1990s, Dr. Martin Brokenleg, professor of Native American studies from 1974 to 2004

SKIING

ca. 1988, Granskou Hall room

1989, Dr. Lansing Prescott, professor of biology from 1969 to 1999

ca. 1991, Augie Doggie

VIKING
DAYS
SIOUX FALLS, S.D.
OCT.20

ca. late 1980s, "The Cottage," the original Model School, served as the home for Augustana's Central Services operation

1996, Government and International Affairs Professors Dr. Dennis Stevens (background) and Dr. Joe Dondelinger lead their popular current events class

of Clay

Sports:
V-ball beats NDSU

ROR

Sioux Falls, S.D.
Thursday, Nov. 7, 1996

d term as president

eer

with the

eceived a
ght before
ot receive
electoral
e Politics
site, only
voting in
r Clinton,
voted for

Clinton's
ppointing.
ave to feel
election."
ined that
o winning
emocratic
ne since
ocrat Lyn-
ved more

ey

campu
a num
I've inv
pus lat
share he
wider au

T pro
grea
and
y to
ong
first
ol-
ff

n
y
lin
J
Exc
Teac
gram
5.
Graduat
ent ch
in
anese
trip a

ges
ectron
ollme

Hum

1999, The Augustana Band tours Korea, Japan, and China under the direction of Dr. Bruce Ammann, professor of music since 1989

ca. 1999, Construction of the Madsen Center

1995, Sandra Zwach '97
first team NCAA Division II
All-America

1991, Julie Krauth '94 leads the softball team
to the NCAA Division II Championship

2000-2006 Dr. Bruce Halverson '66, the only Augustana alumnus to serve as chief executive, is inaugurated on October 6 as the twenty-second president.

Viking Varieties celebrates its 50th anniversary.

James Earl Jones speaks in the Edith Mortenson Center theatre.

Former U.S. Speaker of the House, Newt Gingrich, and PBS NewsHour correspondent, Susan Dentzer, speak at the annual Boe Forum on Public Affairs.

2003

FULFILLING THE MISSION 2000-2010

2000-2001

The first Covenant Awards are given to students who best exemplify each of the College's five core values—Christian, Liberal Arts, Excellence, Community, and Service—at significant events during the academic year.

2001

The September 11 terrorist attacks mark an historic day for Augustana and the nation.

The Fantle Building, housing the Center for Western Studies, is dedicated on December 1.

Augustana begins a partnership with the University of South Dakota's Sanford School of Medicine, participating in the South Dakota Biomedical Research Infrastructure Network (BRIN) grant funded by the National Institutes of Health.

2004

Former mayor of New York City, Rudy Giuliani, is the speaker at the Boe Forum on Public Affairs.

Ground is broken on April 25 for construction of the Center for Visual Arts.

Bob and Kari Hall give $1 million in April for construction of the Hall Football Complex, which will be attached to the south end of the Elmen Center.

The Department of Computer Science is instrumental in the South Dakota Space Grant funded by the NASA EPSCoR [science, technology, engineering, and mathematics] grant.

2005

2006

Ambassador Paul Bremer, former presidential envoy to Iraq, speaks at the Boe Forum on Public Affairs on April 6.

The Center for Visual Arts is dedicated on September 29.

2006-present Rob Oliver is Augustana's twenty-third president.

2007

Former U.S. Vice President Al Gore and former President of Mexico Vicente Fox speak at the Boe Forum on Public Affairs.

Augustana hosts the Nobel Peace Prize Forum.

The Hall Football Complex and Sanford Practice Gym are dedicated.

On September 13, an anonymous donor gifts the College $6 million as the lead gift for a $7 million complete reconstruction of the interior of the Mikkelsen Library.

On September 26, Bob and Kari Hall contribute $6.1 million to build Kirkeby-Over Stadium.

In summer, a record 61 students participate in undergraduate-sponsored research.

Kirkeby-Over Stadium, the Soccer Field, and Huether Tennis Centre are dedicated.

Former Pakistani President Pervez Musharaff speaks at the Boe Forum on Public Affairs.

The Department of Physics is successfully funded to participate in physics research at the Deep Underground Science and Engineering Laboratory (DUSEL).

2009

2010 STUDENT ENROLLMENT - 1,820 (1,694 full-time/100 part-time/26 graduate students)

2008

A new Viking logo is unveiled and the Vikings join the Northern Sun Intercollegiate Conference.

Supreme Court Justice Sandra Day O'Connor is the presenter at the Boe Forum on Public Affairs.

The faculty approves a new honor code.

2010

The faculty approves a new master of arts in Sports Administration and Leadership.

The Fidsvaag Bell is removed from Old Main for restoration and is rung ceremoniously at the Sesquicentennial Day Opening Convocation on September 8.

Augustana continues to be acclaimed in *U.S. News & World Report's* annual college rankings as one of the top five schools in its classification and a "great school at a great price." *The Princeton Review* identifies the College as a "Best Midwestern College," and *Washington Monthly* ranks Augustana sixth of 309 baccalaureate colleges nationwide for "advancing social mobility, research, and service" of its graduates.

Former U.S. Secretary of State Madeleine Albright is the Boe Forum on Public Affairs presenter.

2010, Administration building

2000–2010

Fulfilling the Mission

The year 2000, and the years that followed, transformed lives in many ways for many reasons, and rather quickly, or so it seemed. The world was jolted following the terrorist attacks on September 11, 2001, that took thousands of lives. The search engine, Google, became a word in everyone's language. Social media sites, Twitter, YouTube, Facebook, and blogs were literally at everyone's fingertips. An "i" identified must-haves: iPod, iPhone, iMac, and the iPad. Electronic book readers came on the market and cell phones morphed into smartphones practically overnight. Telecommuting, allowing flexibility in work locations and hours, was introduced. Development of hybrid cars and energy sources, such as wind and solar power, advanced. The issues of climate change and global warming were being debated. The United States elected its first African American president, Barack Obama, who would take office facing an economy that was labeled the worst since the Great Depression. And educational institutions were jumping into the fray to meet the demand for the rapidly developing interest in online learning.

Because of budget constraints, the Wagoner era, which continued into the new millennium, was a time of academic retrenchment. The College focused on its core mission of serving primarily undergraduate students aged 18 to 22, most of whom lived on campus. An adult learner program was scaled back significantly and the Midwest Institute for International Studies, begun in 1982, was eliminated.

2010, The Center for Western Studies, Fantle Building

Early in the 2000s, as higher education became more of a norm, Augustana was faced with an ever-increasing competition for students. It became apparent to College officials that enrolling part-time students—long a staple of the annual enrollment picture—would become more difficult. South Dakota's regental universities had begun expanding dramatically into Sioux Falls in the '90s where many of Augustana's part-time students resided. Concurrent with the lower tuition offered by state schools, other regional private colleges and universities identified Sioux Falls as a prime target for their degree-completion and graduate programs.

However, the College continued its aggressive approach in the search for excellent and diverse new faculty to deliver the academic program. Faculty were generally hired in tenure-track positions only if they possessed an earned doctorate and, as a result, there were notable increases in the research productivity of young scholars who chose to begin their academic careers at Augustana. Many achieved distinction and scholarly competence as researchers and publishers of articles and books—and as presenters at professional meetings.

President Wagoner resigned effective in Summer 2000 after leading Augustana for seven years. His presidency had been one of renewing the spirit of the College and creating a positive campus culture. Building rapport among the administration, faculty and staff, and the students was his priority—and he was hugely successful. The face of the campus had changed dramatically with new and renovated facilities—the Madsen Center, the Edith Mortenson Center, a retrofitted and refurbished Humanities Center, the Nelson Service Center, and the Wagoner Student Street. Following a successful fund-raising effort, ground was broken for the Fantle Building to house the Center for Western Studies. The $31 million Augustana Renewal campaign, initiated in 1995, concluded after raising $40 million.

At a retirement program hosted by the College, Wagoner received the 2000 Chief Executive Leadership Award from the Council for Advancement and Support of Education [CASE] Mid-America District VI, an award given to heads of campus institutions for outstanding efforts in promoting and supporting education and institutional advancement. He also received the Royal Norwegian Order of Merit "for outstanding service in the interest of Norway." Dr. Wagoner went on to serve as president of the Lutheran Educational Conference of North America, a voice for Lutheran and American church-related higher education.

Arriving from his previous post as dean of the School of Theatre at Florida State University in Tallahassee, Dr. Bruce Halverson '66, the only Augustana alumnus to serve as president, was inaugurated in October 2000, as part of the Viking Days Homecoming celebration. Halverson had graduated *cum laude* with majors in speech and drama, and earned his doctorate in theatre history from the University of Washington, Seattle. In his inaugural address, he said, "Augustana will sustain our communities by providing leaders of faith and integrity. We want to send them to your neighborhoods, to live lives of Christian faith, service, excellence, and commitment . . . Augustana radiates like the sunrise on the Northern Plains because our students offer the strongest hope for the glory of the new day."

During the 2000-2001 academic year, members of the Augustana College Student Association convened to give further definition to the College's set of core values: *Christian, Liberal Arts, Excellence, Community,* and *Service.* The open, inclusive process produced the Augustana College Covenant, a living document designed to inspire and guide Augustana students toward more complete understanding of the rights and responsibilities accompanying membership in the College community. During the year, the first Covenant Awards were presented to students who best exemplified the core values.

On September 11, 2001, the Augustana community paused with the rest of the nation and the world to take in the magnitude of the massive terrorist attacks in New York and Washington. "A Year of Dedication" was proclaimed when the Center for Western Studies moved into the new Fantle Building in December. The move expanded important services to the College and the larger community—to preserve and interpret the history and cultures of the Northern Plains. Home to more than 400 artworks, 40,000 books, and the archives, one of the largest collections, given by Lyndon and Shirley King, consists of American Indian portraits by Belva Curtis, depicting the historic struggle between American Indians and white leaders over the American West.

Augustana became a partner institution with Sanford School of Medicine at The University of South Dakota, participating in the South Dakota Biomedical Research Infrastructure Network [BRIN] grant funded by the National Institutes of Health. The federal BRIN grant, designed to build research infrastructure and a culture of research, allowed stipends for biology and chemistry faculty and students to conduct research as well as to purchase state-of-the-art equipment. Later, the Augustana Biology Department would begin the BRIN Phase II research program with increased collaborations among the South Dakota BRIN universities and commercial health care partners. At the end of the decade, the BRIN Phase III was launched which allowed Augustana to bring on new faculty members to mentor students conducting research.

The research culture at the College has long been strong. It developed in the 1950s with grants for equipment that could be used in undergraduate coursework and scientific research. In the '60s, a strategy was adopted to hire faculty to conduct research and to teach, greatly enhancing students' educational experiences in the natural sciences. Relationships have reached into the Sioux Falls community linking the College with facilities such as Sanford Research, Avera Research, and the Sioux Falls VA Medical Center, allowing Augustana students to experience opportunities firsthand that prepare them for entry into their fields of study. The Department of Physics is currently funded to participate in research at the Deep Underground Science and Engineering Laboratory (DUSEL) at the former Homestake gold mine in Lead, South Dakota, and Augustana has been selected to participate in a new center at the University of South Dakota that will conduct research in the fields of astrophysics and nuclear physics.

Boe Forums on Public Affairs were held annually. Guests included Her Majesty, Queen Noor of Jordan; U.S. Speaker of the House Newt Gingrich; Mayor of New York Rudy Giuliani; U.S. Vice President Al Gore; Vicente Fox, president of Mexico, and his wife, Marta; Pervez Musharaff, Pakistani president; and Supreme Court Justice Sandra Day O'Connor. Nobel Peace Prize Forums were held on the Augustana campus in 2002 and 2007.

Diversity in student interests, talent, and outreach were in evidence. Campus ministry extended to South Dakota's Pine Ridge Indian Reservation, inner-city New York, and Mexico. Augie Green, an eco-conscious club for students spearheaded a project to make taxi bikes available on campus. Old bicycles were refurbished and placed in various bike racks for use by students. Expansion of Elmen Center was under way to add space for team locker rooms, offices, and a weight room. The *Mirror* carried commentary on what colors to wear to men's basketball games, and included the question, "Why can't there be just one color?" President Halverson said, "Eliminating one school color is not an option. Augie's school colors have been blue and gold ever since I can remember. I bleed blue and gold. It's out of the question—absolutely not, no way."

In October 2003, Viking Varieties celebrated its 50th anniversary. In its infancy, Viking Varieties showcased the talents of students, faculty, and alumni. It evolved into a near-professional production, appearing in several venues, with attendance reaching into the thousands a time or two. Viking Varieties continues to be a high point of Homecoming festivities.

Musical ensembles continued to tour the United States and internationally. The Augustana Band has participated in performing tours of China three times since 1995 and toured Egypt in 2011. The Augustana Choir has also toured internationally, most recently to Italy and Sicily in 2008. These trips highlight Augustana talent and performers serve as ambassadors, encouraging high school students to consider attending the College.

Mid-decade, the Department of Computer Science, as part of a multi-institutional collaboration, was instrumental in the South Dakota Space Grant Consortium, which offered opportunities for South Dakotans through education, research, and public service in the fields of aerospace, and earth and space science. Funded by a NASA EPSCoR grant, the multiyear project enhanced science, technology, engineering, and math participation and preparation through robotics education and competitions for middle school, high school, undergraduate, and graduate students. In 2010, Augustana received a National Science Foundation EPSCoR grant to fund

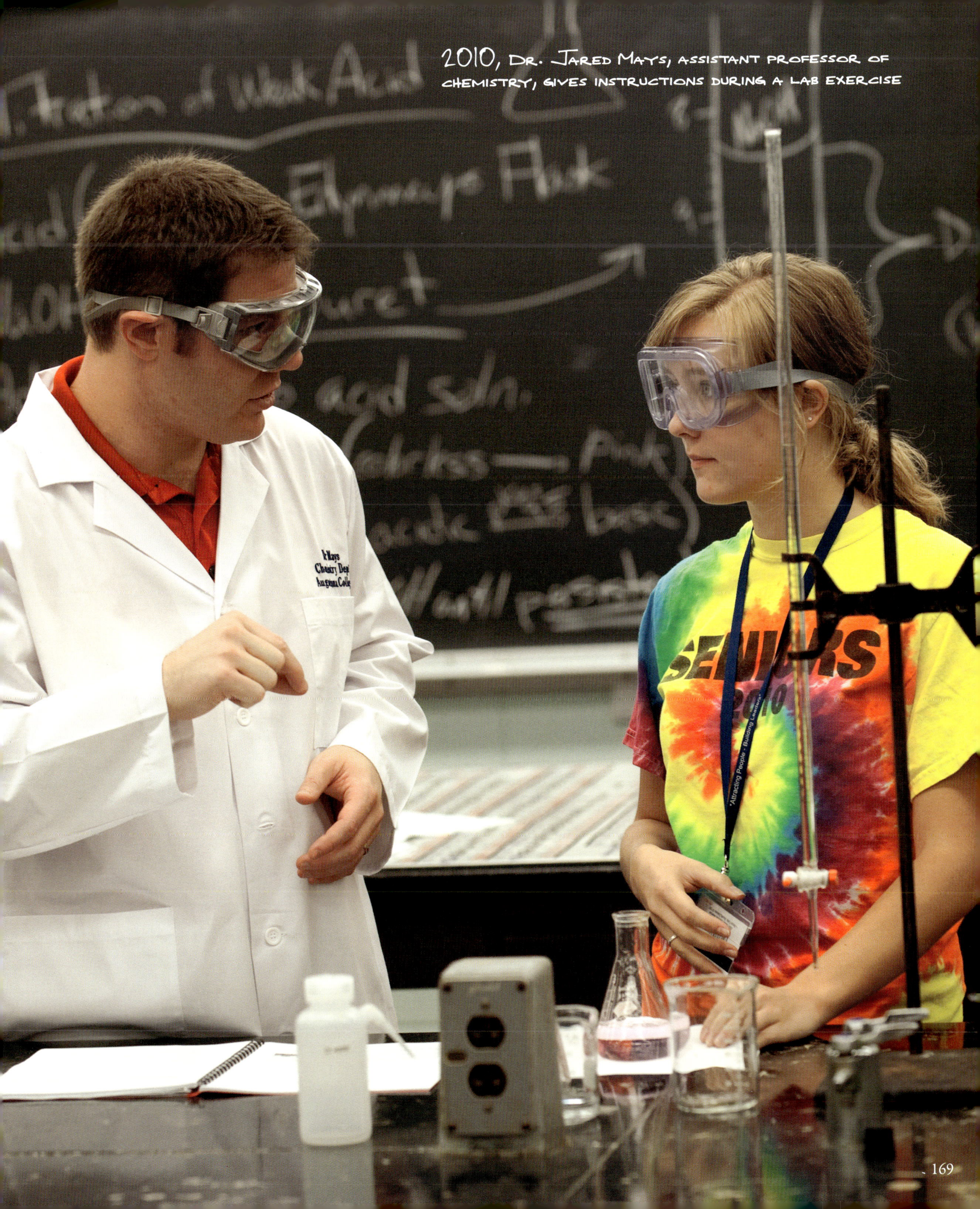

2010, Dr. Jared Mays, assistant professor of chemistry, gives instructions during a lab exercise

2009, The Vikings take the field for their first game in Kirkeby-Over Stadium, a 38-16 win over Emporia State, Kansas

undergraduate research stipends and equipment for chemistry, physics, and computer science. The nursing major, one of Augustana's largest, was experiencing a shortage of qualified faculty—in sync with the shortage nationwide, as an aging nursing population moved toward retirement and fewer students entered the profession.

President Halverson worked tirelessly to balance the budget and to create new funding opportunities for the endowment and facilities. An addition to the Elmen Center was completed. Ground was broken for construction of the Hall Football Complex and the Center for Visual Arts. The Huddle was completely remodeled. The College enhanced its relationship with Our Savior's Lutheran Church, Sioux Falls, as it became home to the Campus Learning Center for Children [day care]. Dr. Halverson was also instrumental in negotiating the move of Sioux Falls Seminary to a new facility across the street from the College. He led the effort to raise $50 million for the Sunrise Campaign, actually exceeding the goal by $14 million. In South Dakota, he was central to securing state scholarships, known as South Dakota Opportunity Scholarships, for students attending private colleges. Upon announcing his retirement from the presidency, Dr. Halverson noted, "I believe my role is, and has been, that of a transitional president."

When the Board of Trustees announced in January 2006 its decision to name Robert C. Oliver as Augustana's 23rd president, the response from the campus and Sioux Falls communities was overwhelmingly positive. Rob Oliver was no stranger to either community; his leadership and passion for life and learning were hallmarks of his career. Oliver served on the Augustana Board of Regents for 12 years. His background was in financial services but, following his interest in higher education, he retired from banking in 2004 and joined the Augustana faculty as an associate professor and chair of the Department of Business Administration. While his tenure within the department was brief, his dedication to students and excellence in the classroom were well known. As president elect, he commented, "It is my wish that every single student will be able to say, 'Augustana is special to me.'" At his inauguration in October of 2006, President Oliver outlined his vision for Augustana saying, "By describing and clarifying our dreams and then passionately sharing them with others, I believe we can successfully assemble the resources we need to fuel our engine of growth with quality. It is my experience that people are eager to invest where they see opportunities for great returns. Augustana is a place where the returns are indeed priceless."

Among Oliver's first tasks was to lead the College through the application process for membership in the Northern Sun Intercollegiate Conference following an extensive study of a 30-member Athletic Advisory Committee. The move was precipitated by the impending disintegration of the North Central Conference. The last season of North Central competition would be during the 2007-2008 academic year. In 2008, as the Vikings joined the Northern Sun, a new, cutting-edge logo of Ole the Viking was unveiled—bearing little resemblance to the 35-year-old "squatty bod" logo.

Augustana introduced a new way to deliver its academic program by offering summer courses online, supported by the philosophy that the College would maintain curricular and quality control if students took courses offered by Augustana, while, at the same time, increasing and diversifying its revenue stream and providing summer work for its faculty. The Global Education House roused the consciousness of global citizenship among students. A decision was made to enlarge the staff in the International Program Office due to a record international enrollment.

Luther House of Study, a collaboration between Augustana and Sioux Falls Seminary, was developed to offer courses to educate students on the teachings of Martin Luther, particularly those interested in going into Lutheran pastoral ministry to supplant the imminent retirement of a major portion of South Dakota's ordained Lutheran clergy. The Hovland Center for Liturgical Arts came into being as a resource for students, the community, and clergy and congregations initiating building or remodeling projects or exploring ways to enhance the liturgical arts in their houses of worship. The College was founded as a mission of the Church. Worship and outreach to area congregations have always been central in campus activity.

The College received a lead gift of $6 million from an anonymous donor toward a $7 million complete reconstruction of the interior of the Mikkelsen Library in 2007. Bob and Kari Hall also contributed $6.1 million to build Kirkeby-Over Stadium, a football-only facility, in honor of Kari's parents. The tennis complex, Huether Tennis Centre, was funded in part by a naming gift from Mike and Cindy Huether. In response to these gifts, President Oliver said, "By adhering to our mission and values, we continue in the tradition of the *Augustana Like Always*, and through the willingness to dream an exciting vision for the future, we are now beginning to glimpse the *Augustana Like Never Before*."

The Sesquicentennial year, 2010-2011, started on a high note with the College recording the highest retention of first-year students; full-time student enrollment at its highest in three decades; record enrollment of international students; and the average ACT composite of the new class the highest on record. The faculty approved a new master of arts degree in Sports Administration and Leadership. The Eidsvaag Bell was removed from Old Main for restoration and was rung ceremoniously at the Sesquicentennial Day Opening Convocation on September 8. Nearly 40 descendants of James Wahl attended the festivities with Augustana sophomore, Kelsey Ramstad '13, ringing the bell that her great-great-great-grandfather safeguarded for Augustana.

President Oliver declared a fresh dynamic when he said that Augustana now understands itself as fulfilling a mission to the Church and seeks to serve as a resource for all aspects of congregational ministry and outreach. As the College celebrates its Sesquicentennial, it remains committed to its partnership with the Church and is determined to nourish the collaboration.

The Augsburg Confession, or Augustana from the Latin, *Confessio Augustana*, is the primary Lutheran confession of faith. The very name, Augustana, recalls the faith and mission of the founders of the College as they put down roots in a new land and forged onward toward educating their constituency, often facing what must have seemed to be insurmountable challenges. The spirit of the pioneers may have wavered, but their faith did not. Augustana is who she is today, thanks to all of the pioneers throughout the years who stood the tests of the times.

2010, Carli Ellwein and Jamie Martin, Viking Days royalty, light the candles on the Sesquicentennial birthday cake at coronation

AUGUS
COLL
TOP-FLITE
NCAA

2001, Volleyball team, coached by Kim Sudbeck '91, takes second place in the NCAA Division II national tournament hosted by Augustana

Dr. David O'Hara, assistant professor of philosophy since 2005

Dr. Sandra Looney '62, professor of English since 1964

Dr. Julie Ashworth '75, assistant professor of education since 2002

2006, Eide/Dalrymple Gallery, Center for Visual Arts

2007, "URINETOWN," DIRECTED BY DR. IVAN FULLER, PROFESSOR OF THEATRE SINCE 1989

2009, The Trustees Scholars travel to Greece

2009, Residence hall
life in The Towers

AUGUSTANA COLLEGE
1860
1889
A
V D
M A
Ω
1918
SIOUX FALLS S.D.

ca. 2008, Commencement and the faculty gauntlet

2009, Fans pack the Hall Forum at the Elmen Center to watch the Vikings beat Northern State

2008, New Viking logo unveiled

2010, Students in the newly renovated Mikkelsen Library

V
I
K

2010, Viking Days fun at Kirkeby-Over Stadium

2009, Aerial view of campus

Restoring the Eidsvaag Bell

A poem to celebrate 15 decades of history

On the eve of a mighty civil war,
molten steel was poured
into a bell-shaped emptiness, hissing,
as it filled the void. Down the street,
a lava of steel made cannonballs and bullets.
Each foundry brought out wooden mallets
to crack open their cores, to show the world
what had been formed in the darkness—
from one foundry: a bell with a tongued clapper,
from the other: gunpowder and oblivion.

After soldiers fell like stalks of wheat
and our hemorrhaging borders were sutured together,
the bullets were lost to history, the cannonballs
were melted down into ploughshares,
but the bell was raised in a tower—ropes groaning.
Land stakes were driven into soil
and hammers clanged against steel.

This is how a college is born.

The bell, like a blind hourglass,
meditated above it all, waiting.

Fifteen decades later,
I watch students rush to class,
they pass through other students who wear
bowler hats, some dance the Charleston,
others worry about withered crops and dust storms.
Many have war memories locked in their closets,
others wear tie-dyes, their feet sandaled like Jesus.
Still others skateboard past, their legs pumping,
pumping, pumping, toward imagined selves.
Their skin is a foggy presence here,
they wiff down the sidewalk, gliding now
through other souls just like them.

Meanwhile, trees open their budded fists,
and professors like me grow old
on this island of youth and ambition.
Like that bell, we know the truth:
that it all blends together,
that on these footpaths ghosts pass through ghosts,
migratory birds come and go, leaves fall, snow melts,
green shoots poke up from the ground, that same ground
where land stakes once banged home,
and a bell—a bell that has been forgotten—
finds its voice again. It magnetizes the air.

Dr. Patrick Hicks
Augustana Writer-in-Residence
Associate Professor of English/Journalism
Presented on Sesquicentennial Day
September 8, 2010

The Eidsvaag Bell

Following its official founding on June 5, 1860, Augustana College quickly and rightfully earned its nickname given by historians, "The College on Wheels." Less than a decade after settling into its first home in the basement of Chicago's Norwegian Lutheran Church, Augustana would move to Paxton, Illinois, in 1863, then in 1869 to Marshall, Wisconsin.

In its first year in Marshall, a local Norwegian farmer named Endre Endresen Eidsvaag quietly donated a 1,000-pound brass bell to the school. An immigrant from Norway, Eidsvaag had arrived in the United States in 1851 and settled in Deerfield, Wisconsin, a small community close to Marshall. Little is known about Eidsvaag—including why he chose to donate the bell, reported to have cost $400. Other than his obvious connection to the Lutheran Church, perhaps he was inspired by the tenacious spirit of the school's founders or maybe he believed in the mission of educating teachers and pastors. Eidsvaag's son, Nils Boe, was a pioneer pastor and his grandson, L. W. [Lars Wilhelm] Boe, would eventually be named the fourth president of St. Olaf College, Northfield, Minnesota.

The records of the Niles Works Bell Foundry, Cincinnati, Ohio, where the bell was apparently cast, have been lost over time. The foundry operated only between the years of 1860 and 1869, meaning that casting of the bell coincided with the formative years of Augustana. It is certainly the oldest artifact of the College—more than 140 years old, and possibly 150. It is fitting then that we use it to celebrate significant events of the College today, as in the past.

The story of the bell is in and of itself intriguing. By the late 1870s, Augustana's leaders found themselves lured to the western frontier. With the strong encouragement from Norwegian James Wahl, a commissioner of immigration for the Dakotas, the school's leaders made the decision to move to Beloit, Iowa. Wahl was given authority by the Church to

2010, Eidsvaag Bell is removed from Old Main

When morning came, students and railroad authorities helped Wahl get the school's possessions to the railroad station for the move to Beloit, with the bell being successfully transported to the depot to be boarded on the train west. However, the sheriff appeared at the rail siding with replevin papers, impounding the bell. A two-year legal battle, led by James Wahl, ensued over whether the bell should remain or go with the school. It seems Porter, having no case and sensing Wahl's unflappable resolve, finally gave in and the bell was allowed to travel to Beloit in September 1883, with Porter actually paying the freight.

move the school and all of its property from Marshall to Beloit so, in 1881, school officials began making arrangements to move the school which, of course, included the Eidsvaag Bell

The people of Marshall, however, had other plans. They believed Augustana's possessions, including the bell, belonged to and should stay with the school building. Led by William Porter, an influential local millionaire, local residents and merchants refused to help Wahl with supplies for the move. With help from the railroad, Wahl procured what he needed from other sources and overcame attempts to stop the move. The bell was removed from its tower and rested on the ground awaiting delivery to the rail depot the next day. A group of men gathered near the gates of the school grounds, intending to abscond with the bell and toss it into a mill pond. Ever vigilant, Wahl became aware of their scheme and spent the night seated on top of the bell, waiting until daylight to transport it safely. Noting Wahl's unwavering commitment to his task of protecting the bell, the locals finally gave up and dispersed.

In 1884, the bell followed Augustana to Canton, Dakota Territory, and finally to Sioux Falls, where it was installed in the bell tower of Old Main in 1918.

For more than 60 years, the signature sound of the Eidsvaag Bell signaled the beginning and ending of classes and commemorated major Augustana events. However, after the weathered and aging Old Main was officially retired from classroom use in the 1980s, the bell was no longer rung.

The Eidsvaag Bell serves as a symbol of Augustana's history and endurance. In honor of Augustana's Sesquicentennial, college officials removed the Eidsvaag Bell from Old Main on June 21, 2010. For the first time in 92 years, the bell saw the light of day. The bell was reintroduced on September 8, 2010, to students, faculty, staff, and alumni at Opening Convocation.

Initial plans call for it to ring out at important and special college events throughout the 2010-2011 academic year before a permanent home on campus is identified. In the meantime, the bell rests in the Center for Western Studies.

Cheers
TO AUGIE YEARS!
HOMECOMING 1948
Augustana
It's a Great Day to be a Viking!
AUGUSTANA COLLEGE, SIOUX FALLS, SD
AUGUSTANA VIKINGS
Viking Days
Oct. 15-17
Augustana College
Augustana
Home Coming
VIKINGS VS HURON
October 17, 1925
Viking Days
Oct. 18-20 1985
VIKING DAY
OCT. 9 1937
VS
HURON
LUTHERAN NORMAL SCHOOL
Oct. 4 - 6
AUGUSTANA COLLEGE
VIKING DAYS '94
October 7 - 9